W9-AMA-328

# Uncle Arthur's
# BEDTIME
# STORIES
## Volume One

# Uncle Arthur's Bedtime STORIES

## Volume One / Arthur S. Maxwell

*Dedicated*—First of all to my children, all six of them—to Maureen, Graham, Mervyn, Lawrence, Malcolm, and Deirdre—from whom came the ideas and the inspiration for so many of these stories. And then to my millions of nephews and nieces all over the world who have read and loved these stories in years gone by, and to the millions more who yet may read them, the boys and girls of every nation who love a story.

Published jointly by

REVIEW AND HERALD® PUBLISHING ASSOCIATION
Washington, DC 20039-0555
Hagerstown, MD 21740

PACIFIC PRESS PUBLISHING ASSOCIATION
Boise, ID 83707
Oshawa, Ontario, Canada

PAINTING BY HARRY BAERG

Copyright © 1976 by the
Review and Herald Publishing Association
Washington, D.C.
Library of Congress Catalog Card
No. 74-83676

Copyright © 1964, 1965, 1966, 1967 by the Review and Herald
Publishing Association.

All rights reserved. No part of its literary or pictorial contents
may be reproduced without permission from the publishers.

Printed in U.S.A.

# Contents

# Lesson Index

7

Artists participating in the illustration of this volume are: Harry Anderson, Harry Baerg, Robert L. Berran, Fred Collins, Wm. Dolwick, Thomas Dunbebin, Arlo Greer, Russell Harlan, Joe Hennesy, Wm. M. Hutchinson, Manning de V. Lee, Vernon Nye, B. Plockhorst, Jack White, and Charles Zingaro. Cover by John Steel.

# Just Between Us

"Please tell me a story, Mamma! Won't you tell me a story, Daddy?"

How often have fathers and mothers heard these imploring words, backed by eager, longing, wide-open eyes that will never take No for an answer.

What can be done about it? Nobody in the world could suddenly think up enough stories for all.

That is how *Bedtime Stories* came to be written. Years ago, when two little children were tugging at his heartstrings for more and more stories, Uncle Arthur began to think of writing some especially for them. So the first little book came out; then another and another, until there were forty-eight in all, containing more than a thousand stories. Millions of copies have been sold in nearly twenty languages.

Now the publishers have compiled some of the best stories in this beautiful new set, full of fascinating color illustrations. In this new format they can go on and on, reaching new generations of boys and girls as the years roll by.

For those who have never seen Uncle Arthur's *Bedtime Stories,* the publishers would like to say that they are different from the usual run of children's storybooks. They are books with a purpose, designed not only to entertain but to build character; to lead boys and girls to choose the good way of life; to help them to be kind, honest, truthful, and obedient, and above all to love God with all their hearts.

Readers may rest assured that every story is true to life. By watching his own children, talking with thousands of other people's children, and reading letters received from boys and girls all over the world, Uncle Arthur was able to write these stories, and every one contains some uplifting, character-building lesson. These lessons are listed in the unique index on page 7, which parents and teachers will no doubt find helpful.

THE PUBLISHERS

◀ Color Photo, T. K. Martin
**Uncle Arthur was never so happy as when in the company of children. These are with him in beautiful Golden Gate Park, San Francisco, California.**

# STORY 1

# Wilfred's Secret

"I WISH I COULD be a pirate!" said Wilfred. "Everything is so dull, and I want to do something exciting."

"Yes," said Gwen, "do let's find something to do."

It was vacationtime. School had been closed for ten days, and the children were getting tired of their playthings. They wanted something new.

"Of course, we can't be pirates," said Gwen, "because we'd soon be arrested."

"Of course," said Wilfred, "but can't we think of something?"

"Let's think."

So they thought and thought. Neither of them spoke for several minutes. Then Wilfred jumped to his feet.

"I've got it!" he cried. "Let's call ourselves the Surprise Package Company. I'll be the president, and you can be the secretary."

"All right, Wilf," said Gwen, willing to do anything her big brother suggested, "but what are we going to do?"

"Do? Why, give people surprises."

"What sort?"

11

◀ Painting by Vernon Nye

The president and secretary of the Surprise Packet Company make a call on one of their customers.

"Oh, good ones, of course," said Wilfred. "We'll find people who need things done for them, and then make them wonder how the things happened. I think we'll get lots of fun out of it."

"So do I," said Gwen. Let's begin soon."

"O.K. I'll make a list of things, and then we can decide which to begin with."

Wilfred found a pencil and paper and made his list.

"Now, see here," he said solemnly, "don't tell anybody what we are planning to do. It's a secret."

"Of course not," said Gwen. "What do you think I am!"

That same afternoon when Mother returned from town she put her grocery bags on the kitchen table. Then she dropped into a chair and stared. What a kitchen! After dinner she had had to go out hurriedly, leaving all the dirty dishes in the sink. Now they had disappeared. The kitchen had been tidied up, everything was in its place, the table was all set for supper, and, yes, even the windows had been cleaned!

All was quiet and still. Nobody was in the house. What kind person could have done all this?

Wilfred and Gwen came in from the garden. Mother asked them whether Auntie had called during the afternoon. Wilfred said No, he didn't think so, but it did look as if someone had been busy.

"Well," said Mother, "isn't it just lovely! I have no more work to do today, and I can have a nice quiet rest this evening! I wonder who did it all."

Mother opened a letter she had found on the mat when coming in. It read:

"The Surprise Package Company called this afternoon

on a little matter of business."

"I wonder what that means," said Mother.

"I wonder," said Wilfred.

"Let's have supper," said Gwen.

And they did.

The next morning two children might have been seen going down the street leading to the little home of Mrs. O'Higgins, a poor, bedridden old lady for whom nobody seemed to care.

The boy, who was holding something in his right hand, knocked gently on the door. There was no answer. The boy peeped in at the window. Mrs. O'Higgins was fast asleep. Quietly opening the door, the boy walked in, followed by his sister. Tiptoeing across the room, the boy placed the package he was carrying upon the table beside the bed and went out. In her excitement the little girl fell over the doorstep.

"Gwen, do be careful!" said the boy.

The noise had awakened the old lady.

"Who is that?" she called.

But the door was shut, and the two children were scampering away as fast as their legs would carry them.

Mrs. O'Higgins picked up the package. It contained three eggs.

"What a mercy!" she said to herself. "But who sent them?"

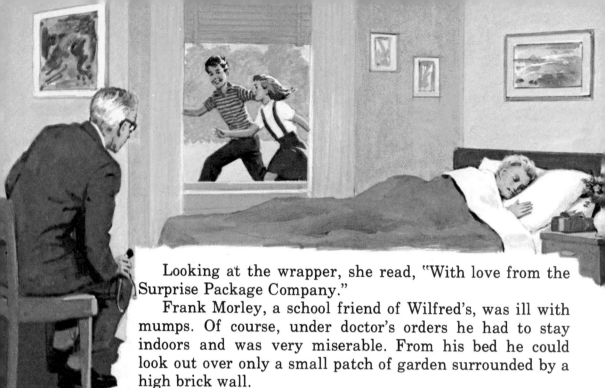

Looking at the wrapper, she read, "With love from the Surprise Package Company."

Frank Morley, a school friend of Wilfred's, was ill with mumps. Of course, under doctor's orders he had to stay indoors and was very miserable. From his bed he could look out over only a small patch of garden surrounded by a high brick wall.

One afternoon he was gazing vacantly out of the window when all of a sudden he saw a square box topple over the garden wall and slide down to the ground, held by a stout string.

"Mother, quick!" he called. "Do see what's in the garden."

Mother, all surprised, brought the box in, and Frank opened it. Inside were four smaller packages. One was labeled, "Open Monday"; the second, "Open Wednesday"; the third, "Open Friday"; the fourth, "Open Sunday."

Since it was Monday, Frank opened the first package. It was a box of paints—just what he had been longing for! Frank thought he had seen the box before but did not know where. Inside the box were the words:

"With best wishes from the Surprise Package Company."

"Whatever is that?" asked Frank.

Nobody knew.

On one occasion the Surprise Package Company was caught.

Wilfred and Gwen were paying a second visit to Mrs.
O'Higgins.

This time they had taken with them some flowers, as well as eggs. As quiet as mice they crept in, placed their gifts upon the table, and departed.

The children were so eager to get in and out without awakening the old lady that they did not notice a man sitting quietly in the next room. It was the doctor.

No sooner had the door closed behind the children than he went across to the table, picked up the package, and read the note:

"With love from the Surprise Package Company."

"So this explains what the old lady has been talking about!" he said. "And now I can understand what Frank Morley told me yesterday."

And this explains, too, how it came about that a few days later a letter arrived at the home of Wilfred and Gwen addressed to the Surprise Package Company and containing an invitation to lunch at Dr. Brown's.

The children had a wonderful time at the doctor's, and there were two surprise packages that made up for all they had given away.

Of course, the children could not understand how the doctor had come to know about their secret, and he wouldn't say a word. It was all a delightful mystery. Wilfred and Gwen were as happy as children could be. Wilfred said that it was much better than being pirates.

# STORY 2

# The Hollow Pie

ROBERT HAD THE VERY bad habit of always taking the biggest and best of everything for himself. His brothers, Charlie and Ted, would call him all sorts of names for doing it, but that did not seem to make any difference.

Mother was very sorry about it, too, especially since Robert, when invited out to parties, always disgraced the family by his greediness. What could be done? Mother talked the matter over with her sister, who lived on the next street.

A few days later the boys were delighted to receive an invitation to dinner from their aunt. Remembering all the good things they had enjoyed there in times past, they looked forward to the day of the party.

At last the day came and dinnertime arrived—for which Robert especially had been waiting.

The table was piled with good things. What Robert looked at longingly were the cupcakes, jellies, small pies, and chocolates.

Robert's eyes gazed excitedly on the wonderful spread of

tasty dishes. Oh, my! he thought, if only I could attend to
this little matter all by myself!

He looked at everything and made up his mind which of
them he would choose when they were passed around.

When all the visitors had been given their places at
the table, dinner began. They all began with bread and
potatoes and greens in the usual way, but Robert soon got
tired of that. He looked at the plate of small pies, one
whole pie for each person. He wanted that biggest one.
Would he get it in time, or would Charlie get it first?

The pies were passed around. Charlie and Ted took small
ones and opened them. What wonderful centers they have!
thought Robert. Now, if only I can get that big one.

Robert's turn came. The biggest pie was still there, and
of course he took it with joy.

But a disappointment awaited him. As he cut through
the top, the whole pie collapsed. It was hollow!

Poor Robert! Tears filled his eyes, but no one seemed to
notice what had happened. He ate the crust as bravely as he
could and said nothing.

The cupcakes were passed round. Robert thought he was

18    quite justified in taking the biggest this time, seeing that there had been nothing in his pie.

But something was wrong with his cake. It looked all right outside, but the center was bitter. What can be the matter? thought Robert. Auntie was generally a good cook. And then, too, the others didn't seem to be having any trouble at all. It wasn't fair, thought Robert, but he didn't dare say anything for fear the others would laugh at him.

Nobody seemed to notice Robert's unhappiness, and no one passed him anything to make up for his bad luck. In fact, the others all seemed to be enjoying themselves to the full.

The chocolates came next, and by this time Robert was getting desperate. "I'll have to make up for lost time by taking those two big beauties in the center," he said to himself as he removed the two largest, best-looking ones from the plate.

"Ugh!" said Robert, groaning inwardly and blushing all over with disappointment. "What a horrible taste!"

Swallowing one with difficulty, he tried the other to take the taste away, only to find it worse.

On the way home Charlie remarked to Robert about the splendid dinner they had had.

"Splendid *what?*" said Robert.

"I thought you weren't enjoying yourself," said Charlie; "you looked uncomfortable. What was the matter?"

"Matter?" said Robert. "Everything I took was bad, even when I took what looked best every time."

"Maybe that was the cause of the trouble, Robert," said Charlie knowingly. "I think if I were you I'd leave the biggest and best-looking things for somebody else next time."

That night Robert stayed awake quite a long time. There were two reasons. One was a pain under his pajama jacket, and the other the advice Charlie had given him. He put two and two together and at last decided that the best and safest course for him would be to follow Charlie's suggestion in the future.

# 3

# Peter Pays Up

PETER WAS STAYING with his grandma, and early one afternoon she suggested that they go shopping together. Peter was delighted. Very soon the two were on their way.

On arriving at the neighborhood grocery store, they went inside and were met with a cheery "Good afternoon" from Mrs. Green, the smiling saleswoman behind the counter. Grandma went over to talk to her and buy the things she had written down on her list while Peter wandered around looking at all the goods for sale.

What a lot of beautiful things there were! In one corner, under a glass case, there was a pile of fresh brown loaves of bread, and the most tempting cakes and pies. In a refrigerator there were cartons of milk and packages of butter and cheese. Piled up on shelves there were all sorts of bright-colored cartons. In the center of the floor were baskets of fruit and vegetables. Altogether they made a very pleasant picture, and the mixture of delicious aromas made Peter very, very hungry.

Maybe you know how it feels to be five years old, to take     21

◀ Painting by William Dolwick

**Five-year-old Peter's love for blackberries got him into trouble, and taught him a lesson he never forgot.**

a long walk, and then go into a store full of food. Well, Peter felt just like that.

It so happened that among the baskets of fruit there were several filled with big luscious blackberries. How Peter did love blackberries! He never could get enough of them, and now here in front of him were more than he had ever seen before.

He put out his hand to take one, but a little voice inside him seemed to say, "No, Peter; you mustn't do that; that would be stealing." But the berries looked so delicious that he felt he *had* to take one. After all, he thought, there were so many, many berries that nobody would ever notice if he was to take just one.

So Peter did not listen to his conscience. Instead, he put out one hand and took just one blackberry. But that one tasted so good that he decided to take another one. How sweet it was!

Then, seeing that there seemed to be just as many left in the basket as there had been before, he took one from another basket. And another. In fact, he was just getting settled to a real meal of blackberries when he heard a familiar voice from the other side of the store.

"Peter! Peter! Where are you?" called Grandma.

"Here I am, Grandma," cried Peter, wiping his hands on the back of his trousers and hurrying around the pile of baskets.

"Come along, dear," said Grandma. "We're all ready to go home now. Would you like to carry one of the bags? How good you have been all the time while Grandma has been shopping!"

Peter blushed a little at this as he took the bag Grandma handed to him. Then they opened the door and went out.

As they walked along Grandma suddenly stopped.

"Peter," she said, "look at me!"

Peter looked up, trying to appear as innocent as possible.

"What are those black marks on your face, Peter?" asked Grandma.

"What black marks?" asked Peter.

"All around your mouth. Not quite black, but blackish red."

"I don't know," said Peter, although if he could have seen his dirty face, he would have owned up right away.

"Peter, you have been eating blackberries," said Grandma. "Haven't you?"

Peter's head went down. "Just one or two," he said.

"Where did you get them?" asked Grandma.

"In the store," said Peter.

"Did Mrs. Green say you could have them?"

"No."

"Do you mean you took them without asking?"

"Yes."

"Then Peter was a very naughty boy," said Grandma, "and I am very much ashamed of him. Come along, let's go home, and we will see what should be done about it."

Peter began to cry, and it was a very sad walk they had together, so different from the journey they had taken but a little while before.

When they got indoors Grandma took Peter on her knee and told him how very wrong it is to take things that belong to other people; that it is breaking the commandment which says, "Thou shalt not steal." She also told him that there

were just two things he had to do. One was to ask God to forgive him and the other was to go to Mrs. Green, pay her for the berries he had eaten, and tell her how sorry he was that he had taken them.

"I don't mind asking God to forgive me," said Peter, crying; "but I don't want to ask Mrs. Green."

"I know it's hard," said Grandma; "but it's the only way. Now go and find your purse."

"You mean I have to pay for the berries myself?"

"Surely you must," said Grandma.

"But it will take all my money," said Peter.

"Never mind if it takes all you have," said Grandma. "You must make it right. But I don't think it will take all. In fact, I think a dime would pay for all you ate."

"A whole dime!" said Peter. "Do I have to give Mrs. Green a whole dime?"

"Yes," said Grandma. "And the sooner you go down to see her the better. Wipe your eyes now and be a big, brave boy."

Peter wiped them with the backs of his hands, and Grandma kissed him good-by. Holding his dime tightly he set off for the grocery store.

How far away it seemed as he dragged one weary foot after the other! But at last the store came in sight and, with his heart beating hard, he went inside.

"What! Back again so soon!" exclaimed Mrs. Green. "Did Grandma forget something?"

"No," said Peter slowly, "I did."

"You did!" said Mrs. Green. "What did you forget?"

"Mrs. Green, er—er—I—er—er—please, I forgot to pay for the blackberries I ate. And—er—er—please, Grandma said they're worth a dime. So I've brought it out of my very own money and—er—er—please, I'm very sorry I didn't ask you about them first."

And with that Peter put the dime on the counter, turned

around, and ran for the door. Opening it, he dashed outside
and started to run home. But he had not gone far when he
heard Mrs. Green calling him.

"Peter!" she said. "I want you a minute. Come back
here."

Very slowly Peter went back, as if expecting to be
scolded.

"You forgot something else," said Mrs. Green, smiling,
and handing him a paper bag.

"No," said Peter, "I didn't leave that."

"But it's for you, anyway," said Mrs. Green. "Just something good for your supper." Then she patted him on the
head and told him to run home quickly. Peter thought he
saw tears in her eyes, but he wasn't quite sure, and he
couldn't think why.

How he did run then! It seemed as though he was home
almost before he had started.

"Look what she gave me!" he cried. "Grandma, look!"

Grandma looked. It was a big delicious-looking doughnut
with jam inside.

"Aren't you glad you went back and made things right?"
said Grandma.

"Am I!" exclaimed Peter.

"It's always the best thing to do," said Grandma.

# 4

# Tinker–
# the Tale
# of a Puppy

"DADDY! DO COME and see what we have found in the garden."

Leslie and Rosie literally dragged Daddy out of the study and into the kitchen, where the queerest, prettiest little pup was wriggling and frisking about.

"Do let us keep him," pleaded Leslie. "He's just a poor little stray thing and wants a home."

"But I've got two puppies already," said Daddy, looking at Leslie and Rosie, "and I can't afford to keep any more."

"Oh, but just this one baby thing," pleaded Rosie. "I'm sure he won't cost much to keep."

"Perhaps he belongs to someone," said Daddy, who didn't want the puppy the least bit.

"Oh, no, we have asked everybody around, and they don't know where he came from."

"Well, you can keep him for a week," said Daddy.

What a joy! They could keep him! He was to be their very own!

Just then the puppy collided with the milk pitcher Rosie had left on the floor beside a saucer, and a moment later a

27

◄ Photo by J. C. Allen

The children became more and more fond of their pet dog, Tinker.

white stream was flowing across the floor and the puppy was licking up the mess as rapidly as his little tongue could manage.

"You bad dog!" cried Leslie. "But I am sure he'll never do it again."

"We'll have to get a good name for him," said Rosie. "Let's call him Tinker." So Tinker he was.

Weeks passed, during which the children became more and more fond of their pet. Tinker grew rapidly, and was soon almost as much a part of the family as the children themselves, although Daddy never seemed quite pleased with having a stray dog in the family circle.

One night, long after everyone had gone to bed, Tinker, who had been put to sleep in the workshop, thought that something was the matter. There was a strange choking smell coming out of the kitchen. He thought he had better call his master, in case something was wrong.

"Yap! Yap! Yap!"

No answer.

The smoke grew more dense, and Tinker barked again. "Yap! Yap! Yap!"

Mr. Norman woke up. "There's that dog barking. Why does he want to wake us up in the middle of the night? I wish I'd never allowed him in the place."

"Yap! Yap! Yap!"

Mr. Norman got out of bed. "Well," he said, "I smell burning wood."

In an instant he was downstairs, and found the kitchen on fire and full of smoke.

Running to the faucet, he threw bucket after bucket of water on the flames, and in a little while succeeded in putting them out, but he was only just in time.

In the morning Tinker was given such a breakfast as he had never imagined in his wildest puppy dreams. As for Leslie and Rosie, they could not love him enough. Daddy went so far as to say that but for Tinker they might have lost their home and even their lives.

From that day he always said Tinker was the most wonderful dog he had ever known, and Mother said, "What if we hadn't let Tinker stay!"

STORY **5**

# Nellie's Wish

SCHOOL WAS OVER. Vacationtime had begun. Everyone was looking forward to Christmas Day. How slowly the days seemed to pass! It seemed as if Christmas would never come. Outdoors it was too cold to play, and indoors there seemed nothing to do without forever getting in Mother's way.

"Oh, what *can* we do?" said Nellie to her sister Elsie.

"Let's write that letter to Santa Claus we were going to send him."

"If you want to," said Nellie. "But do you know, I believe Santa Claus is Daddy dressed up."

"Do you?"

"Yes. Last Christmas I kept one eye open till someone came into my room to fill my stocking, and I'm sure it was Daddy in his dressing gown."

"But let's write the letter anyway," urged little Elsie.

"Oh, yes; that will be fun, won't it? What shall we ask him to send us?"

"Let's get some paper and a pencil first, so we won't forget anything."

30

"I'll run and get some," said Nellie, and off she went,
coming back in a few minutes with enough paper for a long
letter.

Since Elsie had just learned to write, it was agreed that
she should write the letter, while Nellie sat by to tell her
how to spell the words.

"Before you begin, let's try to think of what we would
like most," said Nellie.

So they talked the matter over very seriously, and decided that they wanted a large number of things. Elsie
was sure she needed a box of paints, a baby doll, a doll
buggy, a ball, lots of candy, oranges, and apples, and a
music box. Nellie had bigger ideas. She wanted a scooter,
some good books with pictures in them, a big box of chocolates, and, above all things, a doll that could talk and move
its eyes.

"I really don't think he will be able to carry them all,"
said Nellie.

"Oh, I do," said Elsie. "He has a big bag."

"Yes, and there is no harm in putting them all down."

So they did. With much care little Elsie wrote the letter,
underlining all the things they wanted most. At last the
letter was finished and ready to be placed in an envelope.
Nellie read it over, all the way from "Dear Santa Claus"
down to "Hoping to see you soon." Then she gave a little
sigh, and put it on the table.

32      "Why, what's the matter?" asked Elsie.

Nellie was silent a moment. Then she said, "I think it is a rather selfish letter."

"Why?"

"Because we have asked things only for ourselves. There's not one thing for anyone else."

"That's right. What had we better do? Must we write it all over again?"

"Oh, no; that would take too long. Why not add a postscript?"

"What's that?"

"Just a few words at the bottom."

"All right. What shall we say?"

"I would like to see some of the poor children at school get some nice things like those we have asked Santa Claus to send us."

"So would I."

"There's Kitty Gordon," said Nellie. "She's such a nice girl, but her mother is so poor that I don't suppose she will get any Christmas presents at all—or nothing worth much."

"Won't she really?"

"I don't suppose so."

"Then let's ask for something nice for her. I'm sure she'd like a pretty doll, too."

"Yes," said Nellie, "put that down. Then the letter will be all right, I think."

So Elsie carefully added the words, "Please see that Kitty Gordon gets a beautiful doll." Then they folded the letter, put it in the envelope, stuck an old stamp on it, and handed it to Mother, asking her to see that it was mailed.

Christmas morning came, and with it all the glorious fun of emptying stockings and examining the presents that were piled up under the tree. Nellie and Elsie were as happy as children could be, shrieking with delight as each package was opened and they found something for which they had

asked in their letter. Of course, they did not get *all* their requests; but enough to make them feel sure Santa had read their message.

But there was one thing wrong, at least so far as Nellie was concerned. She did not say anything about it till she had opened all her packages. Then she began to look just a little bit worried. She turned all the tissue paper over again and again and looked under the bed, even in the closet, but in vain. The thing she wanted most of all was not there.

"What's the matter, Nellie?" asked Elsie. "Haven't you got enough things?"

"Oh, Elsie," said Nellie, "I know I have some lovely things, but *it* isn't here."

"What do you mean?"

"Oh, I did *so* want a baby doll that says, 'Mamma.' "

"Maybe he took one to Kitty Gordon instead of you."

"Maybe so," sighed Nellie. "But I didn't really mean him to do that."

Hardly had she said it when she realized how really mean it was. She had all these beautiful things, and she wondered whether Kitty had anything. All day she felt

Painting by Joe Hennesy ▶

**Just as she received the doll she wanted so much, Nellie glanced at the window. There was Kitty Gordon, peering in.**

unhappy about it, and in the midst of the play with her new toys, she kept thinking, "Should I have taken Kitty some of my things?"

In the evening Nellie and Elsie went to a party that was being given by the woman next door. There were several other little girls there, and they had a fine time together. After refreshments—and what good food it was!—they all went into another room, where there was a beautiful Christmas tree covered with pretty shiny decorations and little colored lights. It was a very thrilling sight.

But the thing that took Nellie's attention most was the beautiful doll as it lay among all the other gifts placed beneath the tree. Her heart beat fast as she thought that perhaps now her great wish was to be granted. They played all kinds of games around the tree, and at last the presents were distributed. Only one thought was in Nellie's mind— who was going to get the doll? Impatiently she waited and waited while every other child received a gift. Now there was just one present left beside the tree. It was the doll.

"This," said the woman, "is for——"

"Nellie," said all the children, for they saw that she had had nothing from the tree so far.

Nellie blushed and jumped up from her seat. Taking the doll from the woman, she hugged it tightly to herself.

Then a strange thing happened. Nellie was walking back to her seat when suddenly she pointed to the window and cried, "Oh, look! look!"

Everybody looked, but there was nothing to be seen. The shades were up, but outside all was dark and still.

"What was it?" cried all the children.

"It was poor little Kitty Gordon. She was looking in at the window, and I'm sure she was crying. Oh, I must go and find her!"

Without another word Nellie rushed to the front door and ran out, not even waiting to put on her coat. Far down

the street under a light Nellie thought she saw a little
figure.

"Kitty!" she cried. "Kitty! Come here."

But Kitty went on, and Nellie had to run the whole length of the block before she caught up with her little friend.

"Oh, Kitty!" she panted. "I've brought you something. Please do stop and take it."

Kitty stood there in the street looking in amazement at the wonderful thing she held in her arms. It was a doll that could shut its eyes and say "Mamma."

"For me?" she said.

"Yes, yes, for you," said Nellie. "I want you to have it most of all." Then she turned and ran back to the house, feeling happier than she had ever felt before.

That night before she went to sleep she remembered the note she had added to her letter to Santa Claus, and was thankful she had helped to answer it.

STORY **6**

# Who Was Jesus?

WHO WAS JESUS? A baby in Bethlehem? Yes. A carpenter's boy in Nazareth? Yes. A kind man who helped sick people? Yes. Jesus was all of these, and much more.

Long before Jesus came down to this world as a baby in Bethlehem He lived in heaven.

In fact, He was the One who created this world in which we live. He made the beautiful trees, the flowers, the hills, the valleys, the birds, the animals, and the fishes in the sea.

In heaven all the angels loved Him and delighted to do His bidding. There all was happiness and joy.

Why, then, you ask, if He was so happy in heaven, did He come down to the world at all?

Because He loved the people here, and it made Him sorry to see so many dear little boys and girls growing up to be wicked men and women. True, it was a great sacrifice for Him to exchange the joys of heaven for the sorrows of earth, but He did it, knowing that there was no other way to help people to live better and no other way to save the little children for His kingdom.

39

◀ Painting by Harry Anderson, © Review and Herald

**Jesus is the friend of every boy and girl everywhere.**

Painting by Harry Anderson, © Review and Herald ▶

**"May I hold Him?" the girl asks Jesus' mother eagerly.**

But why did He come as a little baby, and not as a grown-up man?

Just so that He could grow up like all other little boys and girls. He wanted to live as they live, so He could be better able to help them all afterward.

Well, Jesus the baby grew into Jesus the little boy, and He became Jesus the man of Nazareth, who went all over Palestine doing kind deeds and healing all the sick people who came to Him.

He taught the people many beautiful lessons, and told them how to live peacefully and happily together. It was Jesus who said that we should do unto others as we would like them to do unto us.

"You have heard that it was said, 'You shall love your neighbor and hate your enemy.' But I say to you, Love your enemies and pray for those who persecute you" (Matthew 5:43, 44, R.S.V.).

In His own life Jesus carried out these beautiful lessons,
and all the people loved Him. That is, all except a few.
There were some who were jealous of His popularity, or
did not like the way He rebuked them for their sins, or did
not understand Him.

Some of the leaders plotted to kill Him. Think of it!
Here was the Son of the great God of heaven, walking
around among men, healing and helping them in every way
He could, and yet some wanted to take His life!

And these men succeeded in their plan. They told false
tales about Jesus to Pilate, the Roman governor who ruled
Palestine. Pilate was too big a coward to stand up for Jesus
against His accusers. So he sent Him away to be crucified.
The Roman soldiers nailed Him by His hands and feet to a
wooden cross in the cruelest possible way, standing the

cross up on a place called Golgotha, outside of Jerusalem.

There on the cross Jesus soon died, killed by pain and sorrow. When He was dead His friends came and, taking Him from the cross, buried Him in a rock tomb belonging to a man called Joseph of Arimathaea.

You ask, "Why did Jesus let the wicked people kill Him?"

By that He showed them the full extent of His love. He could have called all the angels of heaven to help Him fight against those wicked men who nailed Him to the cross. But no, He was willing to die, for by His death He opened the kingdom of heaven to all who should believe on His name. That is what the beautiful text means that says, "God so loved the world that he gave his only Son, that whoever believes in him should not perish but have eternal life" (John 3:16, R.S.V.).

So Jesus died and was buried, but He did not remain dead. On the third day the disciples came to His tomb and found it open and empty. A little while after, Jesus met them, and they rejoiced that their beloved Master was alive once more.

For forty days He stayed with them telling them of the work He wanted them to do and how they were to go forth into all the world to tell everybody they met—men and women, boys and girls—how much He loved them all.

Then one day while He was talking with His disciples near Bethany He began slowly to move away from them, rising higher and higher into the air until at last, far up in the skies, "a cloud took him out of their sight" (Acts 1:9), and He was gone.

Yet though Jesus went back to heaven He did not forget those whom He left behind on earth. Nor has He ever forgotten His children through all the long years that have passed since that time.

His love never changes. He is the same yesterday, today, and forever. He died when He was only a young man, and He never grows old. Having been a boy Himself once, He

46     knows just how to help other children today, rich or poor, sick or well, in all their difficulties and in all their temptations. He will never fail you if you put your trust in Him. He is the children's Friend.

"There's a Friend for little children
    Above the bright blue sky;
A Friend that never changes,
    Whose love will never die.
Unlike our friends by nature,
    Who change with changing years,
This Friend is always worthy
    The precious name He bears."

STORY **7**

# Those Prayers
# of Yours

DOES JESUS REALLY HEAR and answer children's prayers?

Of course He does, and don't you ever let anybody try to persuade you that He doesn't.

I'm quite sure about it, because, you see, I've had so many children tell me about their prayers that have been answered. Of course Jesus answers children's prayers! There can't be any doubt about it.

I love children very much, but Jesus loves you *all* much more than any fathers or mothers or uncles could possibly love you.

One time Jesus was talking with His disciples about prayer, and He said, " 'Ask, and it will be given you; seek, and you will find; knock, and it will be opened to you' " (Matthew 7:7, R.S.V.).

But that isn't all. He went on to say, " 'What man of you, if his son asks him for a loaf, will give him a stone?' " (verse 9, R.S.V.).

Of course not, you say. It would be a pretty hardhearted father who would give his hungry little boy a stone to eat.     47

◀ Painting by Wm. Hutchinson

One day while Jesus was talking with His disciples He began to rise above the earth higher and higher, until a cloud hid Him from them.

All right. Then He added, " 'Or if he asks for a fish, will
give him a serpent?' " (verse 10, R.S.V.).

There isn't a father on earth who would do anything so mean, is there? Think of giving a child a snake to play with!

Then Jesus added these wonderful words of love: " 'If you then, who are evil, know how to give good gifts to your children, *how much more* will your Father who is in heaven give good things to those who ask him?' " (verse 11, R.S.V.).

This is the measure of His love for us: *How . . . much . . . more!*

It seems to me that in these simple words Jesus is trying to tell us that He loves us so much that there isn't anything, great or small, that He will not do, if it is for our good, if we will but ask Him for His help.

So let us go on saying our prayers, children, believing that Jesus is more ready and willing to answer than we are to ask.

If you are in need, do not worry. He loves you with an everlasting love—a love high as the heavens and deep as the sea.

Do you need something ever so badly, something that seems too big to ask for? Never mind. You cannot surprise Jesus.

And if what you ask for might not be the right thing for you, or might harm someone else, He will give you something else that is better still. He will surprise you with the greatness of His goodness and His love.

To love Jesus is to love the kindest Friend that ever was. Praying to Him is like talking to a dear friend.

He answers every prayer that comes to Him and especially the prayers of children.

It is true that He understands our thoughts afar off, and that He knows our needs before we tell them, but don't you think He prefers us to tell Him in our own simple words just what is on our hearts? I am sure He does.

◄ Painting by Robert Berran, © Review and Herald

**Praying to Jesus is like talking to a friend who loves us very much.**

Now don't get the wrong idea. God will not give us everything for which we ask. Your mother doesn't, does she? If you were to ask her for a five-dollar bill to spend on candy, would she give it to you, even if she could? I should say not. And why not? Because she knows that so much candy would probably make you very ill. So don't be surprised if now and then there does not seem to be any answer to your prayers. When that happens ask yourself this question: Was that a selfish prayer I made? God does give us things, sometimes, that are just for ourselves, but He doesn't want to spoil us any more than Mother does. He is more likely to answer our prayers when we ask help for others.

And now I think we are ready to answer our first question, which as you will remember was, Does Jesus really hear and answer children's prayers? He does. Not always in the way we expect, but in some way that is best for us. No sincere prayer goes unanswered.

Do not let yourself become sad or discouraged if you do not get an answer to a prayer right away. If you are sure that what you want is good—good for you or good for somebody else—keep on praying. God may just be testing your faith—to see how much you trust Him. Remember, of course, when you ask God for something, always say, "If it be Thy will." Then, whatever happens, you will be satisfied. If you trust God like this you will never be worried if the answer seems slow in coming or if it doesn't seem to come at all.

In the next story, and in other stories in these volumes, you will read truly amazing examples of answers to prayer —children's prayers, too. I have been collecting them for some time, and I am acquainted with all the people concerned. Of course I have not given their real names, or the real places where the events happened, for they might not like that, but the stories are true.

When you read the first of them, I am sure you will say, "That was remarkable." When you read the second, you will say, "That was amazing." But when you have read them all, I believe you will say, "That makes me sure now that God does answer prayer."

Yet there is only one way to be perfectly certain, and that is to prove God for yourself. Ask Him for something yourself—something that you really, truly need, or, better still, something for someone else. Ask Him earnestly, seriously, confidently, and then wait and watch.

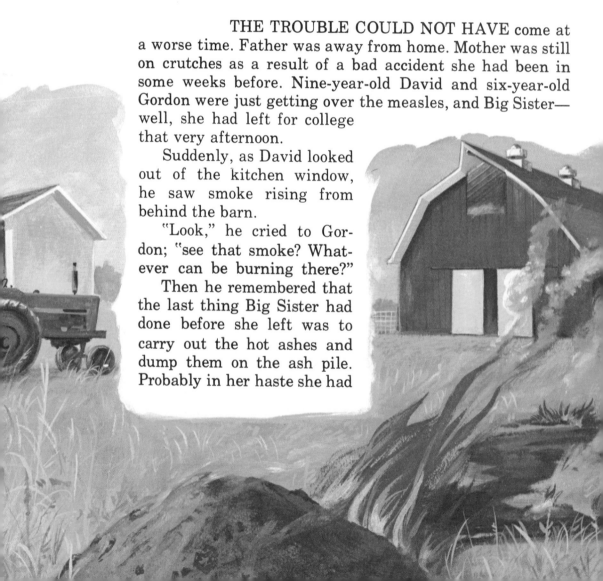

STORY **8**

# Two Brave Firemen

THE TROUBLE COULD NOT HAVE come at a worse time. Father was away from home. Mother was still on crutches as a result of a bad accident she had been in some weeks before. Nine-year-old David and six-year-old Gordon were just getting over the measles, and Big Sister—well, she had left for college that very afternoon.

Suddenly, as David looked out of the kitchen window, he saw smoke rising from behind the barn.

"Look," he cried to Gordon; "see that smoke? Whatever can be burning there?"

Then he remembered that the last thing Big Sister had done before she left was to carry out the hot ashes and dump them on the ash pile. Probably in her haste she had spilled some on the dry grass.

"Fire!" he cried. "Fire!"

"What's on fire?" cried Mother from the next room, hobbling out on her crutches.

"Look, Mother!" cried David. "The grass is on fire near the barn and the flames are spreading fast. See the smoke! Oh, what can we do?"

Poor Mother had never felt so helpless in all her life. Everything she owned was in danger, and yet with her injured foot she could do nothing.

"David, run for water, dear. Quick, quick!"

"Yes, Mamma," cried David, grabbing two pails and running to the stream, which was at least fifty yards away.

Gordon grabbed another pail and in a flash was following his brother. Quickly they filled the pails, hurried back, and poured the water on the burning grass nearest the barn. Then back for more water, and back again to the fire.

54    But it seemed a losing fight. After all, how could two little boys with three little pails put out a great big fire?

"Keep it away from the gas tank!" cried Mother. "See, it's going that way."

It was. Nearer and nearer it crept to the precious store of gasoline Father used for his tractor. If that should catch fire, then the house, barn, and everything might go.

The boys were getting tired now. It was so far to the stream! And it seemed farther every time they went down to it. Still they ran as hard as they could, and with every step they kept praying that Jesus would help them put the fire out.

Back they came with water to save the gas tank. And they saved it—just in time. Of course, they couldn't hope to stop the fire from going across the field—not with their three little pails—but they tried—oh, so hard—to keep it from creeping over to the barn and the house. And they won! The farm was saved.

Just as things were at their worst and the boys were getting so tired that they felt they couldn't carry another pailful, the wind changed, blowing the fire down toward the stream, where finally it burned itself out at the water's edge.

Was Mother proud of them? I should say she was! And so was Father, too, when he got home and learned of all they had done.

As for David and Gordon, they told me that they were sure they managed to beat the fire because of the little prayer they had prayed so often as they hurried to and from the stream with their pails.

STORY **9**

# New Hearts
# for Old

I HAD WANTED A REALLY GOOD radio-phonograph ever so much for quite a long time. Then one day I heard that a man who owned one of the finest stereo sets ever made was selling it because he was leaving the country. I went to see him, and as soon as I heard its beautiful tone I knew it was the radio of my dreams. We finally agreed on the price, and the stereo became mine.

Two days later a truck drew up at my house and two men staggered in with the beautiful new piece of furniture and placed it carefully in the corner of my dining room.

I plugged it in and began to turn the various knobs.

There were grunts and squeaks and groans and roars and rattles, but no music. Try as I might, I could get nothing out of that beautiful cabinet but dreadful groans and shrieks as if it were full of evil spirits. What could I do?

At last I called in a friend who understands radio.

But the same thing happened to him. As he turned the knobs, the set roared and rattled as before.

"How about your tubes?" he said after a while. "I think they are worn out or have been jarred on the journey."

55

"If that's the trouble," I said, "get some new ones."

I shall never forget watching him take the old tubes out and put the new tubes in. Then he switched on the electric current again, turned the knobs ever so carefully, and——

Ah! all was different now. Out from the set came the most glorious music I had ever heard, distant and unearthly at first, but swelling into loud, majestic tones that fairly shook the house.

My dream had come true, although before it was possible I had had to change the tubes.

And do you know, whenever I think of that experience, my mind goes to that text in Ezekiel in which God says, " 'A new heart I will give you, and a new spirit I will put within you; and I will take out of your flesh the heart of stone and give you a heart of flesh' " (Ezekiel 36:26, R.S.V.).

It seems to me that we are all very much like that stereo of mine, beautiful on the outside but bad on the inside—or like a beautiful-looking doll that was given to a little girl one time. Just as the little girl was hugging the doll and kissing its pretty face, its eyes fell in! And then it looked so ugly that she felt she could never love it anymore.

Sometimes it happens this way with little boys and girls. Perhaps Mother will dress her children in nice new clothes so that they look so clean and spotless that people think they are almost little angels from heaven. But they begin to quarrel, and there is such a noise and such a squabbling that they become more like monkeys or wildcats than children—let alone angels!

It isn't just clothes and looks that make people beautiful. There are lots of little girls with lovely curly hair who can be as cross as bears when they can't have their own way.

And there's many a little boy looking very fine in a new suit who can be as stubborn as a mule when he chooses.

Have you ever read the story of David, the brave, honest little shepherd boy? He had a beautiful face, so the Bible tells us, and he was beautiful inside too, for he had a good heart.

And God chose him to be king, " 'for the Lord sees not as man sees; man looks on the outward appearance, but the Lord looks on the heart' " (1 Samuel 16:7, R.S.V.).

As long as our hearts are stony we are like the radio with old tubes inside. It will be impossible to get any good music out of us. Stony hearts produce nothing but grumbling and growling, naughty words and sullen mutterings, and everything that is unkind and unholy.

If you hear a boy being disrespectful to his father, or cross with his brother, or rude to his mother, you may know that he has old tubes inside and needs to have them changed.

Or if you hear a girl finding fault with her food, or her clothes, or her friends, or saying cruel, cutting words to members of her family, you may be sure that she needs new tubes.

It's the failure to get the tubes changed that causes all the trouble.

Why don't we do it? It doesn't cost anything at all. God has promised to do it for us free of charge. Look at the text again. Notice what God says:

"A new heart I will give you."

That's clear enough, isn't it? And so is the rest.

"A new spirit I will put within you."

"I will take out of your flesh the heart of stone."

"And give you a heart of flesh."

God's offer is perfectly plain. And it is open for every one of us to accept.

And if we do, what a change will come over us! Mother won't know us, for sure. And Daddy will hardly be able to believe his ears. There will be such beautiful music—such loving words, such tender sympathy, such gentle answers, such willingness to help and lift and share.

When Jesus comes back to this earth again—and He is coming very soon—to take His children to the wonderful home He is preparing for them, He will not bother much about their looks, you may be sure. What He will ask is, Does this child love Me? Is he a good boy? Has this little girl given Me her heart?

If boys and girls—and men and women—do not love Him, He will have to leave them behind. He simply couldn't take them into His beautiful kingdom and let them spoil it for everybody else. That is why He " 'will send his angels, and they will gather out of his kingdom all causes of sin and all evildoers' " (Matthew 13:41, R.S.V.).

We don't like to read about that; it doesn't sound nice. But then, we do not need to have that happen to us. Jesus wants us all to live with Him in His beautiful home, and He has done everything to make this possible. All He asks is that we love Him and ask Him to change our hearts and make us beautiful inside and help us to be more like Him every day— like Jesus as He was when He was a child and then as He was when He grew up. Then when He comes we'll hear Him say to us:

" ' "Come, O blessed of my Father, inherit the kingdom prepared for you from the foundation of the world; for I was hungry and you gave me food, I was thirsty and you gave me drink, I was a stranger and you welcomed me, I was naked and you clothed me, I was sick and you visited me, I was in prison and you came to me." . . . "Truly, I say to you, as you did it to one of the least of these my brethren, you did it to me" ' " (chap. 25:34-40, R.S.V.).

This is God's idea of goodness. This is the beauty He loves. These are the beautiful things He wants us to do. Those who do them He will take to the beautiful land where all is peace and joy and happiness, and where cross and ugly things never enter.

# The Two Carolines

CAROLINE HERMAN WAS a very nice little girl in many ways. She had pretty hair and big blue eyes, and when she was all dressed and ready to start out for school you would have thought, to look at her, that there wasn't a nicer little girl in all the world.

But there were two Carolines. One was the home Caroline and the other was the school Caroline. The home Caroline was left on the doorstep every morning and picked up every dinnertime when the school Caroline came back.

Now, the home Caroline was a cross, pouty, grumbly, growly, and disobedient Caroline, quite unlike the Caroline that everybody saw outside and thought was such a nice little girl.

Mother was worried almost to tears over her two Carolines. What could she do?

Now, Caroline loved her schoolteacher very much. Indeed, by the way she acted, it seemed as if she loved her teacher more than she did even her own mother. She would take flowers and other pretty things to her to show her affection, and of course the teacher, seeing only the school

62

◀ Painting by Harry Anderson, © Review and Herald

**Jesus has a beautiful place ready for all who love and serve Him, where they will live in happiness forever.**

Painting by Vernon Nye, © Review and Herald ▶

**Outside of her home, everybody thought Caroline was a sweet, courteous girl. At home she was quite a different person.**

Caroline, thought she must always be a very good girl.

One day the school Caroline came home and changed suddenly on the doorstep, as usual, into the home Caroline. After a while Mother called to her, "Will you please go around to the store and buy me some groceries? Here is the list."

"No, don't want to, I'm tired," snapped the home Caroline.

However, she finally decided to go under protest.

While she was gone, a visitor came to see Mrs. Herman to plan for the next parent-teachers' meeting, and was invited to stay for dinner.

"Just make yourself at home in the living room," said Mrs. Herman, "while I do a little in the kitchen. You can write at my desk and I'll leave the door open so we can talk."

In a few minutes Caroline came into the kitchen, slamming the back door as she entered and grumbling about the
heavy groceries.

"Here are your old things," she said, throwing them
down on the floor. "Now I'm going out to play."

"But Mother's tired; wouldn't you like to help her finish
her work?"

"No, I don't want to."

"Well, please set the table for dinner."

"Don't want to."

"But you must do something to help Mother. Please set
the table, Caroline."

"Oh, I hate setting the table," said Caroline, slamming
the door and putting on a pout that would almost frighten
anyone. Pulling out the tablecloth from the drawer with
many grumblings, she spread it out in a rough-and-tumble
sort of way. Then she brought out the knives and forks,
scattered them among a few dishes, and prepared to walk
off.

Mother looked displeased, but did not say anything until
Caroline was about to go. Then she said, "Caroline, set an

66 extra place at the table. We are having a visitor to dinner tonight. In fact, you might speak to her now. She's in the living room."

Startled, Caroline looked around and noticed that the living room door was open.

"But, Mother dear"—her tone had suddenly changed—"the table is not set for visitors."

"No, but it is set for Mother."

"But, Mother, I would like to arrange it better."

"It is too late now. We must not keep our visitor waiting. Please call her in."

Trembling a little, Caroline went into the living room.

"Mother says, Will you please————"

She stopped. It was her teacher!

"Oh, Teacher, have you heard all I have been saying? Oh, dear!" cried Caroline, bursting into tears.

"I am sorry my little Caroline is not the same at home as she is at school," said Teacher.

"Oh, I'm so sorry!" wept Caroline. "I won't ever be so naughty again."

And, really, to tell the truth she never was.

# 11

# The Boy
# Who Ran Away
# From Home

ONCE UPON A TIME there was a rich man who had two sons.

The man was a good father and loved his two boys dearly. He was willing to do anything for them to make them happy, although, like all fathers, he expected them to obey him and do as they were told.

Their home was well furnished and beautiful. They always had plenty to eat and fine clothes to wear. Out on their broad farmlands they had sheep and goats, cattle and perhaps horses—just what most boys would love to own.

But one of the boys was not happy. He did not like the rules that his father laid down sometimes. He thought he would never really enjoy life until he got away from home.

He had heard that out in the world there was plenty of money to be easily gained. In the big city, too, he would be able to have all sorts of pleasure which he would never be allowed at home. He would be free! There would never be anyone to say to him, "Don't do this," or "Don't do that"! He would be a grown-up man, his own master.

The more the boy thought about it the more eager he was

to leave the old farm and go out on his own. He decided to
speak to his father and tell him what he wanted to do.

"Father," he said, "I am tired of living around this old
place. I want to go out and see the world. Please give me some
money."

Father was upset, but knowing that the boy would never
appreciate home until he had been away from it, he gave him
some money and told him he might go if he wished.

The boy was pleased and excited, and at once packed up
his belongings and started off.

I don't know how he felt the day he left. I presume he was
a little sorry when he kissed his mother good-by and when he
waved his hand to her for the last time as he passed out of
sight of home. I am sure his mother cried when he was gone,
and his father too.

That first night away from home must have been rather
lonely for him. Perhaps he thought of going back, but in the

morning again his mind was full of the great future before him in the world. Just to think of the money his father had given him! He had never had so much in his life before! What he would do with it when he reached the big city!

He reached the city and began to spend his money. At once he made a great many friends, who were only too well pleased to help him spend it. They gave him what seemed to be a very happy time, although it meant doing many things that his father had told him were wrong.

"This is real life," said the boy; "this is what I have always wanted. I can do just as I like, and there's no one to stop me from anything. To think that I ever lived back on that old farm!"

But one day the boy discovered that his money was giving out. He had not been paying much attention to money matters beyond spending. Now it came to him as a great shock that the money he had brought with him was almost gone. His pockets were nearly empty.

His new friends soon discovered this. Then one by one they left him, until at last, when he was penniless, he found that he was friendless too. Not one of his companions was willing to lend him anything or even give him food.

The boy was now face to face with the stern fact that food is bought not with money but with labor. He began to see that if he was to keep himself alive he would have to go to work. But what work could he do? The only thing he knew anything about was farming, and he did not know much about that.

So he went to a farmer and asked for work. The farmer thought he was rather a useless sort of boy, and so gave him the job of looking after his pigs, with very low wages.

Here the boy who a few days before had been strutting about the city like a little lord on his father's money was acting as a pigkeeper on a farm. Indeed, he was so hungry that he felt he could eat even the pigs' food.

Poor boy! He had run away from home to have a good time in the world, but he found at last that the world is a very cold, hard place; and though it gives pleasures for a little while it does so at heavy cost.

Of late he had been too busy pleasure seeking to think much about his home, but sitting there among the pigs he had plenty of time to think.

Home! What a beautiful place it seemed! What would

he not give to be there again! Just to see his father and   71
mother once more! Oh, why had he wanted to run away?

A great resolve entered his heart. He would go back. His
father might be angry with him, but he would tell him he
was sorry and ask his forgiveness. He planned what he would
say to his father when he got home. It ran like this:

" 'Father, I have sinned against heaven and before you; I
am no longer worthy to be called your son; treat me as one of
your hired servants' " (Luke 15:18, 19, R.S.V.).

So the boy started on his long walk back home.

Meanwhile what was happening at home?

The father was miserable. His son had not written to him
once. Somehow he felt sure that the boy would get into

trouble. If so, that might drive him home again.

Every day and many times a day the father would go and look up the road along which the boy must come should he ever return. Day after day he was disappointed.

Then one day he went again to look. Straining his eyes, he peered long and earnestly up the road to where it went out of sight over the hilltop.

What was that? Surely a figure moving. Yes! And strangely familiar. It looked like his long-lost son. Could it be? Could it? "I believe it is my boy," the father murmured to himself, straining his eyes still more. "It is! It is! He has come at last!"

Forgetting his age and everything else, the father was so happy he started to run, never stopping until he had reached the boy.

"Father, I have sinned——" began the boy.

But his father scarcely heard. He was too overjoyed that his boy was home again. Putting his arms around his neck, he hugged and kissed him.

When they got to the house, he called a servant to bring some new clothes for the boy to wear instead of his rags, and very soon there was great rejoicing. Then the father held a big party to celebrate the happy event.

The boy's brother couldn't quite understand why all this fuss should be made over a bad boy's return, but the father said:

"My son was dead, and is alive again; he was lost, and is found" (Luke 15:24). That kind father represents God. He loves us all as His children. If we want to run away from Him, He may allow us to do so, but He knows that if we do we shall have a very sad experience.

All the time we are away from Him He will be looking and longing for us to come back. He loves us with an everlasting love, and is always willing to take us back home again. How much better, though, never to run away at all!

◀ Painting by Vernon Nye, © by Review and Herald

**The boy's father scarcely heard his son's confession, for he was too overjoyed that his boy was home again.**

# 12

# Lazy Laurie
# Became
# Mother's Helper

I WOULDN'T LIKE TO SAY out loud that
Laurie was lazy, because probably he would be very much
offended; and I don't like to offend anybody. But I am afraid
that was the truth.

No matter what it was that you asked Laurie to do he
would always reply, "I can't." For every job he seemed to
have an excuse. If you asked him to bring in a scuttle of
coal he would say, "I can't; it's too heavy." Or if you asked
him to go on an errand he would say, "I can't; I'm too tired."
Perhaps you would ask him to wipe the dishes. Then he
would say, "I can't; that's a girl's job."

Of course, there was nothing at all in any of his excuses,
and I am quite sure that the real trouble with Laurie was
just pure laziness. You see, he said "I can't" only when there
was work to be done. He never said it at playtime or when
his chum came to the door and asked him to go bicycling
or to play ball. Then it was always, "All right, I'll be with
you in a minute."

Laurie's Mother told him many a time that it wasn't fair
74   that he never helped the least bit in the work of the home

and yet was so ready to run off and play. But Laurie was just the same as ever the next day, and all Mother had said did not seem to make any difference. But one day Mother had a bright idea.

The next morning Laurie stayed in bed so long that he was late for school. Usually Mother would call him in good time, only to be answered by a dozy, "I can't get up; I'm sleepy." This morning Mother let Laurie get up when he liked, and that was very late indeed. He was cross when he came downstairs, and wanted to have his breakfast immediately. But there was none for him.

"Why didn't you get my breakfast?" he asked.

"I can't," said Mother with a curious smile. "I'm so tired."

Very angry, Laurie ran off to school without any break-

fast. He was so late that the teacher scolded him in front of the class, which made him crosser still.

On the way home he climbed a fence with some other boys, and coming down found himself hooked on a rusty nail. He managed to get down at last, but left part of his trousers on the top of the fence. When he got home he wanted Mother to mend them at once.

"I can't," said Mother. "I'm too busy."

"And have I got to go back to school like this?" asked Laurie, pointing to the hole in his trousers.

"I'm afraid so," said Mother, and go he had to, greatly to the amusement of the boys and girls.

When Laurie got back from school, of course he wanted his supper at once, for he had not had much to eat that day. But there was nothing on the table. He was greatly sur-

prised, for he had been used to finding everything ready
for him.

"You haven't got the supper ready," he said to Mother.

"No," said Mother; "I can't. I'm tired. I just didn't feel like it tonight."

"But I want to go out to play right after supper," said Laurie.

"All right," said Mother, not stirring from her armchair, and looking back at the book she was reading, "go ahead. I don't mind."

"But aren't you going to get me any supper?"

"I can't; I'm tired."

Laurie stormed out of the house and slammed the door. But as he was going down the street he began to think things over. Perhaps Mother *was* tired after all. Maybe she really did need someone to help her. Perhaps she really was too tired to get her own supper ready.

Laurie stopped. He thought of the game of ball he was going to enjoy and then of his mother sitting at home too tired to get her own supper ready. He began to feel sorry that he had been so cross. He would go back.

Peeping through the kitchen window, Laurie saw that Mother had gone to sleep in her armchair. At once he

realized that this was his opportunity to make things right. At heart he was really a good boy, even though he had that very strong habit of laziness where work was concerned.

Creeping into the kitchen on tiptoe, he washed the dishes as silently as he could, then, still more quietly, crept into the dining room and set the table. To be quite frank, this was the first time for many months that Laurie had set the table, but he made a fine job of it. He put out all the nicest things he could find, brought in some flowers from the garden, and really made the table look as if someone extra special were coming to supper.

Then he noticed that he had forgotten to bring in the butter dish, and went to get it. Unfortunately, it was a little greasy, and it slipped out of his hands, falling with a crash to the floor.

Mother awoke and jumped out of her chair as if something dreadful had happened. She had been dreaming about

Laurie, and the noise had come just as he had been getting into trouble. But her fears were turned to joy as she saw the neatly set table.

"Well!" she exclaimed, "who would have believed you could set a table so nicely!"

They had a lovely meal together, and Mother never said a word about the broken butter dish all evening. Laurie was so happy that he determined that he really would help Mother more after this.

Just as they were finishing supper, there was a knock at the door, and a boy's voice called out, "Come on, Laurie, we're all waiting for you."

"Sorry, I can't come," said Laurie. "I'm going to help Mother this evening."

But Mother overheard, and she came running to the door.

"It's all right, Laurie, this time. You can help me tomorrow."

Overjoyed, Laurie ran off, and my! that was the best game of ball he ever played.

# 13

# The Boy
# Who Brought
# Heaven Nearer

IT ALL BEGAN IN CHURCH in Italy. Forgetting the music and the prayers, a boy kept his eyes fixed on a swinging lamp. Someone had just lit it, then left it swinging freely on its chain.

As the lamp swung to and fro, young Galileo noticed that it took as long to swing in a wide arc as in a small arc. Not having a watch, he timed it with his pulse and found he was right. This was a new thought. He had always supposed it naturally would take longer for a pendulum to cover the greater distance.

As soon as he got home from church that day he fixed up a pendulum of his own, set it going, and found that it worked the same way. Then he made more pendulums of different lengths and weights, hanging them from ceiling beams and boughs of trees till his family thought he must be crazy. But he proved his point. And this started him on the highroad to many another discovery.

Galileo loved to experiment. He wouldn't accept anybody else's say-so, but set out to prove things for himself.

In his day it was taught in the schools that if two weights    81

◀ Painting by Robert L. Berran, © by Review and Herald

Fascinated by a swinging lamp, the young Galileo timed its movements by the beat of his pulse.

PAINTING BY W. F. SOARE          © BAUSCH & LOMB OPTICAL CO.

Through Galileo's telescope they could see the streets of Padua, twenty miles away, and people walking in them.

were dropped from a high place the heavier would hit the ground first. Galileo questioned this. Then he tried dropping weights from high places, and found it wasn't true. All weights released together hit the ground at the same time. But nobody would believe him.

One day he persuaded a group of university professors to go with him to the top of the famous Leaning Tower of Pisa. From there he dropped a ten-pound weight and a one-pound weight together. Both hit the ground exactly at the same moment. The professors were amazed, but preferred to believe their books instead of their eyes!

In 1609 Galileo made his greatest discovery. In this year a rumor reached him that a Dutch spectaclemaker's assistant, holding two glass lenses a foot or so apart, had noticed that they made things appear larger. Immediately Galileo set out to prove whether the story was true. He set up two lenses a foot apart and got the same result. Then he took larger lenses, put them together, and made the first telescope.

News about his invention soon spread, but many people scoffed and said it couldn't be so. Then Galileo took his telescope to the top of the Campanile, the highest tower in Venice. With him went many of the leading people of the city, including senators, all clothed in rich robes as though attending an important ceremony. What they saw astounded them. Through Galileo's telescope they could see the streets of Padua, twenty miles away, and people walking in them. A ship fifty miles away seemed no farther than five miles. Again and again they looked through the telescope and marveled.

After that Galileo began making telescopes for sale. People from all over Europe bought them. The one he made specially for himself he called "Old Discoverer." It made objects appear thirty-three times nearer.

One night—and that was a very great night in history— he turned his telescope on the heavens. The glorious scene startled him. Instead of seeing just a few stars, such as can be seen by the naked eye, he saw thousands upon thousands of them. The Milky Way, which most people had thought of as a misty veil, was revealed as a gorgeous band of stars. Suddenly he realized that the universe was not merely the earth, the sun, the moon, and a few pinpoints of light called stars but something infinitely greater and more marvelous. The darkness of space was lit with blazing orbs as far as human eyes could see!

Galileo turned his telescope on Jupiter and found the three bright stars on a line with it to be not stars at all but moons, moving around the planet, even as our moon moves around the earth.

Looking at the sun through darkened lenses, he saw a great ball of fire with dark clouds moving over it, which today we call sunspots. He noticed, too, that the sun was moving on its axis, just as the earth does.

This was too wonderful. His heart was thrilled. He longed to tell others, and did so. But again many would not believe him. Church leaders told him he must be mistaken. It was all so different from what they had always believed that they were sure he couldn't be right. They had him arrested and put in prison so that he could not teach his "false" ideas.

But Galileo was right, and he knew it. He knew, too, that others would look through the telescopes he had built, and prove that he was right.

And so, of course, it turned out. As years and centuries rolled by, bigger and bigger telescopes were built, each one proving not only that what Galileo taught was true but also revealing that the universe is far greater than even he imagined.

Maybe you have read about the 200-inch telescope on Mount Palomar in southern California, the largest telescope ever built. Someone—perhaps your schoolteacher—will tell you how it helps astronomers to peer billions of miles into

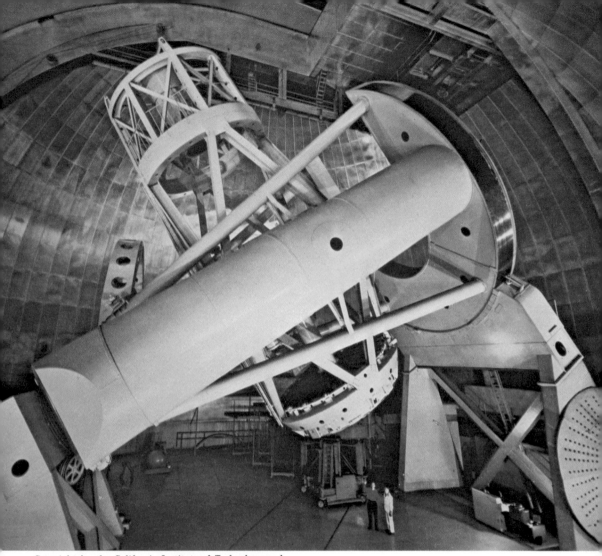

Copyright by the California Institute of Technology and
the Carnegie Institution of Washington

**The 200-inch Hale telescope at the Palomar
Observatory, California, has helped astronomers learn much about the heavens that Galileo did not know.**

space, and how it has revealed many new wonders in the
skies about us. When you think of this, remember Galileo,
the boy who watched the swinging lamp in the church and
who by inventing the telescope opened up the secrets of God's
marvelous universe and brought heaven nearer to earth.

# Diana's
# Donkey Ride

"DO LET ME HAVE A RIDE on a donkey," begged Diana for the fifth time that afternoon.

"No," said Mother. "I've told you, Diana, that you cannot have anything else today. You want everything you see, and if there's a new way to spend money, you find it. So please don't let me hear anything more about that donkey business."

"But, Mommy——" pleaded Diana.

"No!" said Mother, and her voice left no doubt that she meant it.

Diana walked away. Evidently she thought it was no use worrying Mommy anymore. She strolled away toward the donkeys.

There were a dozen of them, all standing together, waiting for children to come and ride on them. Even while Diana watched, a group of children came up, paid their money to the man in charge, and went off gaily along the sands.

There was only one donkey left, and he stood there good as gold even though his master had gone away. Diana went up to him and stroked his nose.

"Dear Mr. Donkey," she said, "you'd like to give me a ride, wouldn't you, if I had enough money?"

"Hee-haw," said the donkey.

"You are a dear," said Diana. "I believe I could ride you all by myself. It must be easy. Look at all those other children."

As Diana looked at the other children she realized that both they and the man in charge of them were a long way off and that she was alone with this donkey.

At once a great idea came into her mind. She would have a little ride after all, even if she only sat on his back and moved around in a circle. Surely the man wouldn't want any money for that.

Nearby were some steps on which the children stood when getting up onto the donkeys' back. Very cautiously Diana led her donkey over to them and climbed up. Nobody seemed to

notice her, and she felt very much pleased with herself.

As for the donkey, he seemed quite used to this sort of thing, and stood there as quiet and gentle as a lamb. Diana was delighted. She was on a donkey at last, even though Mommy hadn't given her any money for it.

Suddenly, however, something happened to Mr. Donkey. He seemed to realize that he had been left behind by the others. While he had been standing alone it had not mattered, but now that he had someone on his back he felt that he should be with his friends. So turning around, he jogged off at a smart pace across the sands.

Diana was never more frightened in her life. What would the man say? She had no money to pay him. And what would Mommy say when she found out?

Gladly would she have jumped off, but she dared not. She took hold of the reins, but the donkey only moved the faster.

Donkeys do not usually run very fast, but to Diana this one seemed to be rushing away with her at a terrible speed. He seemed to hear the others in the distance, and wanted to catch up with them.

Bump, bump, bump, bumpety, bump! On went the donkey, with Diana rolling from side to side, expecting to fall off any moment and almost panic stricken with fear.

"Stop, donkey! Stop, donkey!" she gasped.

But Mr. Donkey had no intention of stopping.

Oh, why didn't I do what Mommy said? thought Diana. This is terrible. Won't he ever stop?

Bump, bump, bump, on across the sands, over the breakwaters, went the donkey, scaring the gulls all along the way.

And now, oh horrors, the donkey was taking her past the very place where Mother was sitting quietly knitting in her deck chair.

"Mommy!" shrieked Diana.

Mother looked up from her knitting. In an instant she took in the situation and started running after Diana.

◀ Painting by Harry Baerg

**The donkey went bumping along, with Diana rolling from side to side, panic-stricken with fear.**

"Stop that donkey!" she cried. "Stop that donkey!"

Other people heard her cry and saw her running. They took up the chase as well. Presently there were more than a dozen people rushing along the sands behind the donkey. As for him, he thought it was one huge joke, and ran faster than he had ever done in his life. Bump, bump, bump!

Poor Diana! What she suffered! She felt sure she would never be able to sit down again.

By this time the other donkeys had reached the end of their course and turned back. The driver soon saw what had happened and came running toward Diana.

"Hi, hi!" he called out angrily. "What does this mean?"

But Diana did not care what it meant.

"Take me off, take me off!" she cried.

He took her off and told her what he thought of what she had done.

And after Mother had paid the driver what he asked for Diana's ride she told her little daughter some things that she will not forget for some time.

And Diana passed a new resolution never again to disobey Mommy.

# Poor Priscilla

"OH DEAR!" CRIED BARBARA, wringing her hands, "what can be the matter with Priscilla? I must get the doctor at once."

Laying poor Priscilla down on her pretty white bed, Barbara picked up her toy telephone and pretended to put in an urgent call to her family doctor.

"Hello! Is that you, Dr. Pills?"

"Yes, madam," came a voice from the other side of the door. "This is Dr. Pills. What can I do for you?"

"Oh, Doctor, my poor Priscilla is sick. Please come at once."

"I will come at once," said the voice in the corridor. "My car is waiting at the gate, so I shall be only a few moments."

Barbara returned to Priscilla's bedside and tried hard to shed some tears over her. There was a knock at the door, and she opened it.

"Ah, so here you are, Dr. Pills. I'm so glad you've come."

Dr. Pills, wearing Father's best hat and carrying his brief case, walked over to the bed. He tried to look serious as he took off his gloves.

"Let me feel her pulse," he said, taking Priscilla's tiny hand.

"Ah, very fast, very fast," he murmured.

"Poor Priscilla!" said Barbara.

"Now let me look at her tongue," said Dr. Pills.

"I'm afraid she's too sick to open her mouth," said Barbara. "Do tell me what you think is the matter."

"A serious case," said Dr. Pills. "Very serious."

"Oh, what shall I do, what shall I do?" cried Barbara wringing her hands.

"Do?" said Dr. Pills. "There is only one thing to do. You must treat the child better. You have been feeding her wrong. She has acute indigestion, and probably will die."

"Die! Oh dear, how terrible!" exclaimed Barbara. "What should I feed her to make her well and strong again?"

"Ahem!" said Dr. Pills. "Let me see. This child has been

eating too much candy. She    93
has been eating it all day
long, and it has ruined her
stomach. You must stop giving her candy except at
meals."

"But she will cry so!" said
Barbara.

"Never mind," said Dr.
Pills. "Better cry than die.
Children must not eat between meals. It is very bad for
them. And, let me see, does she eat plenty of greens?"

"Oh, no, Doctor. She hates greens. Whenever I put them
on the table she grumbles terribly."

"Never mind," said Dr. Pills sternly. "Better grumble
than be ill. She must eat some greens every day—lettuce,
cabbage, sprouts, broccoli, and things like that."

"Not all of them every day!"

"Oh, dear no!" said Dr. Pills. "But one of them at least
every day. And let me see, does the child get enough fruit?"

"She likes bananas and pears, but they are so expensive I can't afford to give her very many."

"She must have plenty of fruit. Stop giving her sugary cakes and pastries, and give her apples and oranges instead."

"I once heard," said Barbara, "that an apple a day keeps the doctor away. Is there any truth in it?"

"Certainly," said Dr. Pills. "I shall *never* have to come back again if you do that—unless, of course, she catches measles or scarlet fever."

"Oh, thank you so much, Dr. Pills," said Barbara. "How much is your fee?"

"My fee?" said Dr. Pills. "My fee is two dollars and a half."

"Rather high, isn't it?" said Barbara, taking two big buttons and five little buttons out of her purse.

"My usual charge," said Dr. Pills. "Thank you. I trust your daughter will soon be better. And be sure you follow my instructions."

"I will," said Barbara as she closed the door. "But, Peter," she called, "you won't forget to put Father's hat back in the proper place, will you?"

# Love Unlimited

I WAS IN AUSTRALIA, traveling by car from Newcastle to Sydney. It had been a very busy day and I was tired, slouched down on the front seat beside the driver, hoping to get a little sleep on the way home.

Then I heard it—the voice of a little girl talking very sadly to her mother.

"Well, I love him anyway," she said.

Instantly I was alert and sitting up. Standing behind me was six-year-old Suzanne looking at her mother on the back seat and talking earnestly about something very important.

"What was that you said?" I asked.

"I love him anyway," said Suzanne, with tears in her voice.

"Whom do you love so much?" I asked.

"My dog," said Suzanne.

"But doesn't everybody love your dog?"

"No," said Suzanne. "My mother doesn't."

"What sort of dog is it?" I asked. "Is it a very big one?"

"No," said Suzanne. "It's just a teeny-weeny pug puppy."

"And your mother doesn't love it?"

95

"No," said Suzanne. "And she wants to get rid of it."

"But why doesn't your mother love your dog?" I asked.

"Because he chewed up her new shoes and tore up some of her clothes."

"Oh, that was bad of him," I said. "What else did he do?"

"He pulled a sheet off the clothesline. And he tore up a newspaper and left the pieces all over the garage."

"Anything else?"

"Oh, yes. When Mother takes the trash outside he brings

it right back. The other day he brought back a whole lot of
melon rinds and piled them on the kitchen floor."

"I can see why Mother doesn't love him very much," I said.
"How about Daddy? Does he love the puppy?"

"He doesn't love him either."

"Why not?"

"Well, you see, just after Daddy washed and polished his
car the other day, my dog ran all over it with his muddy feet.
And was Daddy mad!"

"I can understand that," I said. "You must have quite a
lively little dog."

"Oh, he's bad," said Suzanne. "I know he's bad. And
Mother doesn't love him and Daddy doesn't love him and nobody loves him——"

"Except you," I broke in.

"'Cept me," said Suzanne. "I love him anyway."

Suddenly I thought of all the boys and girls in the world
who are just like Suzanne's little dog. Lively, mischievous,
and naughty as can be—but their mothers love them anyway.

Isn't that the way your mother loves you? No matter what

you do, no matter how bad you get sometimes, she loves you just the same, and will go on loving you as long as you live.

And so with Daddy. You may make him "awful mad" sometimes, but he loves you dearly and always will.

God is like that. He never stops loving us despite all our mistakes. He never gives up hoping that we will be good.

The Bible speaks of the length and breadth and height and depth of the love of God, and says it is beyond our understanding. It is. It is just too big. It is "as far as the east is from the west" and you could never measure that, could you?

God's love is without limit and without end.

Somehow little Suzanne felt the greatness of His love when she said of her naughty dog, "I love him anyway."

# The Secret
# of Happiness

THE RADIO WEATHER REPORT said that snow was coming. This was good news for Joe and Gerald. It set them ablaze with energy.

They had often talked about making sleds for themselves, but so far had never done so. The good news about the snow made them decide to make one each, and so they eagerly began the task.

Every moment they could spare from their schoolwork the boys spent in the shed in Gerald's back yard sawing, planing, hammering, until at last to their great joy the sleds were completed and ready for the snow to fall.

But it did not come. Probably the clouds were blown away after the weather experts had looked at them. However that may be, the sad fact is that for many days there were two sleds in the shed with nothing to slide them on.

School closed for Christmas, and still there was no snow. Day after day went by cold and wet. There seemed about as much prospect of snow as of a heat wave. The boys gave up hope and wished they had never taken the trouble to make their sleds.

99

At last Christmas Eve arrived and with it came a sudden change. The rain stopped, the thermometer went down with a rush, and a strong wind arose.

"Something is going to happen," said Joe, as he went to bed that night. And he was right.

In the morning the clouds had gone, and the rising sun glistened on a vast expanse of snow. A heavy fall had covered the whole landscape with a glorious white mantle—just what they were hoping for.

Gerald was overjoyed. As soon as he awoke he guessed what had happened, for he could see the reflection of the snow on the ceiling. He leaped out of bed, dressed as quickly as he could, and rushed down the garden to the shed where the precious sleds had been stored so long. He hauled them both over the snow up to the house and then ran off to find Joe.

How happy they were! This was better than their highest expectations. No Christmas Day could have started more joyously for them. They decided that they would go off at once to a neighboring hill and have all the fun they had dreamed of.

They trotted off down the street dragging their sleds behind them. School friends shouted to them, all eager to share in the fun.

"Lucky fellows," they cried; "can we have a ride on your sled?"

"Not now," cried Joe and Gerald, "we're going off by ourselves today."

"Lend us one of your sleds," cried another.

"Nothing doing!" shouted Joe. "You should have made one for yourself."

Ralph Morton, the lame boy, waved his hand cheerfully from his window, and wished them lots of fun.

"Nice of him, wasn't it?" said Gerald.

"Yes," said Joe, " 'specially as he can never hope to pilot a sled of his own."

Just then they passed Madge Green's house. They had always been friendly with her and her little sisters. She greeted them cheerfully as usual and wished them a happy Christmas.

"Wish I could come for a slide," she said, "but I can't today. I'm helping Mother all I can, so that she can have a really happy Christmas."

The boys passed on. Soon they were out of the town and climbing the hill dragging their sleds behind them. Then they prepared their slide and the fun began.

Swish! Away they went down the hill. Then up to the top
again. Then another glorious slide. So they played together
for a couple of hours.

After a while, however, Joe noticed a change coming over
Gerald's face.

"What's up, Gerald?" asked Joe with some concern as they
climbed the hill together, this time a bit more slowly.

"Nothing much," said Gerald, "only somehow I'm not getting as much fun out of this as I thought I would."

"Aren't you?" said Joe. "I'm not, either. Of course, it's nice in a way, yet I don't feel comfortable. I wonder why it is."

"Funny we should both feel the same way," said Gerald, "isn't it?"

"Very funny," said Joe, as they trudged on up to the top. Swish! Down they went again.

On the way up next time they talked about their strange feelings again.

"I think I know what's the matter," said Joe.

"What?" asked Gerald.

"I keep thinking about Ralph."

"So do I," said Gerald. "And Madge and the others. I wish we hadn't left them behind. Mean of us, wasn't it?"

"Yes," said Joe.

There was silence again as they climbed slowly upward.

"I think we'll have only one more," said Joe.

"All right," said Gerald.

They had the last slide, and then turned toward home. On the way they talked of how they would spend the afternoon. As they reached the town they began calling at the homes of some of their friends who had no sleds. What Gerald and Joe said to them seemed to make them very happy.

Dinner was scarcely over when there was a loud knock at their front door. Running out, Joe and Gerald found a happy, excited group of children waiting for them.

"Hurrah!" they all cried when they saw the two boys. "I'll be first," said one, and "Me, me, me, first!" called another.

Then sorting the visitors out, Joe and Gerald put two or three of them on each sled, and took them for rides up and down the street. Oh, the shrieks of joy! How they all did laugh and yell!

All the afternoon they kept it up—except for a game of snowball now and then—giving rides to all the children in turn, until at last, too weary to run anymore, Joe and Gerald sent them all home and put the hard-worked sleds back in the shed.

STORY **18**

# When the Well Dried Up

RENE WAS SO THIRSTY. There was not a drop of water to be found anywhere. For many, many days there had been no rain. Not a cloud had crossed the sky, and the fierce African sun had scorched the whole land over hundreds of square miles. The rivers and streams had dried up, and now the deep well close to the farmhouse had run dry.

Rene's daddy did not know what to do. He had worked very hard for many years to build up that home and to develop his land. Now it seemed that he was about to lose everything. His crops were withering away, and worse still, his cattle were parched with thirst, for there was no water to give them. What could he do?

Calling his family together, he told them how serious

the situation was and that he was going to ask Jesus to send rain.

So they all knelt down—Mother, Daddy, Rene, and her baby sister—and together they prayed as they had never prayed before. Father and Mother both prayed very earnestly that Jesus somehow would send rain to save the crops and to spare the herds of cattle.

When it came Rene's turn to pray she did not say just what Mother and Father had said. She said, "Dear Jesus, if You don't send rain, please send some water into the well."

Daddy smiled, because he couldn't see how water could come into the well if it didn't rain. But Rene did not think about that. She

108  believed that Jesus could do anything; and when they all got up off their knees she said she was quite sure that Jesus was going to answer her prayer.

Father and Mother went about their various tasks around the home, but Rene disappeared. She had gone to the well to watch what Jesus would do.

She pulled and pushed at the cover, and finally succeeded in moving it enough so that she could look down. But the well was so deep and dark that she could see nothing at all. Picking up a stone, she dropped it in and listened intently. There was a moment of breathless waiting. Then——"Splash!"

The next instant she was off to the house as fast as her legs could run.

"Jesus has sent the water!" she cried. "Jesus has sent the water!"

Father wouldn't believe it, but came running to the well to see, with Mother and the farm workers close behind. He dropped in another pebble, and there was another splash.

A moment later he had the pump working, and out from the well there was soon pouring a stream of clear, cold water.

How happy and thankful they all were! And do you know, from that day to this, that well has never run dry. Of course, some people say, "It just happened so." But little Rene knows better. She says Jesus sent the water in the well and answered a little girl's prayer, and I believe she is right.

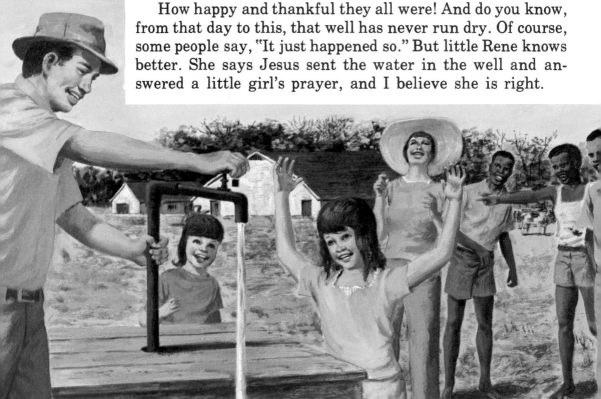

# 19

# Peggy's Extra Present

IT WAS A WEEK before Christmas. Eight-year-old Peggy and her little brother Marcus were shopping with Mother.

Such a happy time they were having! It was great fun buying presents for everybody and spending all the money they had been saving up for the past few months.

Peggy's arms were full of packages. She had a present for Daddy, another for Marcus, and a very special one for Mother. Oh, yes, and still another for Aunt Jane and a teeny-weeny one for cousin Mary, who was only six months old.

Mother had a lot of packages too, and she was standing at a counter in the toy department buying one more present when the worst thing possible happened. Marcus disappeared!

Peggy was the first to notice he had gone.

"Mother!" she called. "Where's Marcus?"

Mother looked around anxiously.

"Marcus?" she said. "Isn't he with you?"

"No. He just ran away. How can we ever find him in this crowd of people?"

109

"Oh dear!" cried Mother. "I can't leave this counter for a moment. I'm in the middle of paying a bill. You go and look for him."

"But I'll drop my packages," said Peggy.

"Put them down here and I'll look after them."

Hastily Peggy put her armful of packages on a stack of books and hurried off in search of her little brother.

"Marcus! Marcus!" she shouted as she dodged between and around the shoppers as they stood in the aisles and crowded around the counters.

She felt pretty sure that Marcus was still somewhere in the toy department, most likely looking at something that had caught his fancy earlier in the afternoon.

She was right. Turning a corner, she saw him sitting in a "spaceship," perfectly happy and without a thought that his mother and big sister were wondering where he was.

"Marcus!" cried Peggy. "You shouldn't run away like this. Mother is terribly worried about you."

Taking him firmly by the hand, Peggy hurried back to Mother.

"Here he is," she said. "Now where did I leave my packages?"

"Over there," said Mother, "on that pile of books. Pick them up and we'll go home before Marcus gets into more mischief."

Peggy gathered up her packages, tucked them as carefully as she could under her arm, and followed Mother and Marcus to the door and so to the bus and home.

"Well!" she cried, as she sorted out her things on the kitchen table. "Look, Mother! I've got an extra present!"

"What do you mean?" asked Mother.

"Why, Mother, look what I've got here!" she cried, holding up a beautiful book of animal pictures.

"Did you buy that?" asked Mother.

"Oh, no," said Peggy. "I never saw it before."

"Then where did you get it?"

"I don't know. I just found it on the table."

"Peggy," said Mother seriously, "you must have picked that up in the shop by mistake."

"Maybe I did," said Peggy.

Mother looked at the book. "It's lovely," she said. "And see the price—$5.95!"

"Just to think I brought home a book like that without knowing it!" said Peggy. "I do hope nobody will think I stole it!"

"What do you think we should do about it?" asked Mother.

"Oh," said Peggy at once, "I'm sure Jesus would want me to send it back, wouldn't He?"

"Yes indeed," said Mother. "And I'm glad you thought of that first. It would be nice if you would write a little note to the manager, telling him how it happened. Then we'll wrap the book up carefully and send it back."

"Maybe I should write the letter now while I'm thinking about it," said Peggy.

"A good idea," said Mother. "And I'll get supper ready."

So Peggy wrote a little note. It read like this:

"Dear Mr. Manager: This afternoon when I was in your shop I picked up a book by mistake with my other packages. I didn't find out about it till I got home. I'm very sorry. And because I didn't pay for it I'm sure Jesus would want me to send it back. So I'm sending it. With love from your little friend Peggy."

Mother read the note and said she thought it was very nice. Then she tucked it into the book, which she then wrapped ready for mailing.

A few days later, just before Christmas—and this is absolutely true—Peggy received a reply to her letter. The manager wrote to say how pleased he was to know that there was such an honest little girl in town. And because she had sent the book back so promptly, he was sending her a little present to show his appreciation.

When the gift arrived it proved to be a pair of beautiful red slippers. They were so lovely, and so unexpected, that Peggy could hardly believe her eyes. She put them on at once and danced all around the house in pure delight. Indeed, every time she put them on she felt a warm glow inside, so glad she was that she had done the right thing and sent that book back!

# Seventeen Cowards

BILL CAME RUSHING into the house and flopped down in a chair breathless. He looked scared.

At that moment Father came in from work. "What's the matter, Bill?" he inquired anxiously.

"Oh, nothing," said Bill.

"Yes there is," said Father. "I can tell by the look on your face. What has happened?"

"Oh, well, Dad," said Bill, wriggling uncomfortably in his chair, "you see, we were all playing ball up there on that vacant lot near Mrs. Boliger's. You know where it is, Dad, about half a mile from here."

"Yes, I know it well," said Father. "I used to play on it myself when I was a boy."

"Well, Dad, the ball——" hesitated Bill.

"I know what you are going to say," said Father. "The ball went through Mrs. Boliger's window."

"Well, yes, Dad. That's what happened. It was an accident, but how did you know?"

"I just guessed," said Father. "But, say, Bill, why are you so scared?"

115

◀ Painting by Manning de V. Lee

Seventeen boys were playing ball on the vacant lot near old Mrs. Boliger's.

"I'm not really scared, Dad," said Bill, "but, you know, Mrs. Boliger is such a mean old woman. She makes such a fuss about things like that."

"Well, what did you all do after the window was broken?"

"We ran away."

"You ran away!"

"Yes."

"Well, how many boys were playing?"

"Seventeen."

"And you mean to tell me that all seventeen of you ran away, afraid of what some elderly woman might say to you?"

"Yes, Dad," said Bill, hanging his head a little.

"Well," said Father, "all I can say is that I think you were just seventeen cowards, that's all."

Bill didn't like that, but he knew in his heart that the charge was true. For a moment he tried to defend himself.

"But, Dad, Mrs. Boliger is such an old crab!" he said.

"It doesn't matter what she is," said Father. "If you boys broke her window, you should have had the courage to go and tell her you did it and offer to pay for the damage. Why, it wouldn't have cost more than a few cents apiece. By the way, who hit the ball that broke the window?"

Bill hesitated. "Er-er-er——" he began.

"Now come on," said Father. "There couldn't have been seventeen balls, nor could seventeen boys have smashed the window at once."

"That's right, Dad."

"Then who hit the ball that broke the window?"

"I did," said Bill, very crestfallen.

"I thought so," said Father, "only I wanted you to own up. And now no matter what the others do you must go at once to Mrs. Boliger's, tell her you are sorry, and ask her how much the damage will be."

"I couldn't, Dad," cried Bill, truly alarmed. "I simply couldn't. She is such a mean old thing."

"But you must," said Father severely. "It is the only proper thing to do. What is more, no boy of mine is going to be such a coward as not to apologize when he has done a thing like this. So get yourself cleaned up, and we'll go."

"You mean you are going with me?"

"Yes, I am going with you as far as Mrs. Boliger's front gate, and then you are going to go to the door and speak to her all by yourself."

"Oh, brother!" Bill muttered to himself as he got off his chair and went to the bathroom to wash his hands and brush his hair.

By and by he came downstairs again, where Father was all ready, waiting for him. Together they set out for Mrs. Boliger's.

It wasn't a very happy journey; at least not for Bill. He couldn't have been more scared if he had been on his way to an examination or to prison.

"Do I really have to go?" he asked after a while.

"I'm afraid you do," said Father. "There's really no other way. And you will feel a great deal happier when you have done the right thing."

Silence fell again. They walked on, Bill wishing that the

distance might have been    119
twenty miles, so Father would
get tired and give up.

At last they turned a corner and came to the vacant
lot where the accident had
taken place. Mrs. Boliger's
house was in full view, and
so was the broken window.

"Here we are," said Fa-
ther, as they reached the little white gate at the entrance
to Mrs. Boliger's property.
"I'll wait here while you go
to the house and speak to
her. It is much better for you
to do this little job alone. I'll
be nearby if you need me."

There was nothing else for
Bill to do now but go on alone,
but as he went up the path
he felt sure that Mrs. Boliger's eyes were watching
him all the way.

And all the time he kept thinking to himself, What will
she say when I tell her I was the one who broke her window?

Bill rang the bell. It sounded loud and long, like the very
knell of doom.

The door opened, and there stood Mrs. Boliger. To Bill's
surprise she was wearing a smile. He had not expected that.

"How do you do?" she said in a kindly tone of voice. "What
can I do for you?"

"Well—er—well—er," stuttered Bill, blushing all over,
"I—er—I—er—am the boy who—er—hit the ball that—er—
broke your window this afternoon, and I'm—I'm sorry."

Bill hesitated and then turned away a little as though he were waiting for a bomb to explode.

But it didn't. Instead, he heard a sweet voice saying, "I am proud of you, son. I have had my windows broken this way many, many times, but you are the first boy who has ever come to tell me about it. You are a real gentleman. You

surely must have been brought up well. You must have a
wonderful father."

"Oh," said Bill, "that's my dad over there. He happened to come along with me."

At this, of course, Father had to come up the path and join them.

"You have a fine boy here," said Mrs. Boliger. "In fact, I think he's the grandest boy I've ever met. You know, sir, no boy has ever come here before and spoken to me like this about breaking my windows."

"Well, Mrs. Boliger," said Father, "Bill and I would like to pay you for putting the glass in again."

"Oh, dear," said Mrs. Boliger. "I'd hate to make you pay when the others never have. I think I have a piece of glass."

Bill beamed. "Then Bill and I will put it in for you," said Father.

They all talked together while the glass was put in place. Then Father and Bill said good-by and started for home.

"I suppose," said Father, "you aren't sorry you went to see her?"

"I should say not," said Bill. "Why, she was as nice as pie. I never would have dreamed that Mrs. Boliger could be like that. I wonder why the boys say that she is mean. She isn't a bit mean. She couldn't have been kinder or more considerate."

"Boys say those things sometimes because they don't understand," said Father. "By the way, Bill, don't you feel better now since you have done the right thing, the brave thing?"

"Do I!" said Bill. "I could jump clear over the moon!"

# 21

# Tom's Slippers

TIM WAS NOT in a very good frame of mind. He was inclined to grizzle—if you know what that means. It is sort of halfway between a cry and a grunt. Little boys get the complaint every now and then, usually when they want what they can't get or when they don't like what they do get.

The cause of the grizzling this time was a paintbox. You see, Tim had a paintbox and Tom, his brother, had a paintbox. Unfortunately, Tom had used up all the paints in his box. He liked to pour lots of water into his paints and then paint big pictures on Daddy's newspapers. So of course his paintbox was soon empty.

That being the case, Tom began to cast longing eyes at Tim's paintbox; and Tim, having painted smaller pictures than Tom, and so having a few paint cups left that were not empty, thought it wasn't fair that he should share them with Tom.

Whereupon there was a strong difference of opinion about the matter. Tom made a grab at Tim's paintbox, and Tim sought to defend his box by jabbing Tom in the nose with his

123

◀ Painting by Vernon Nye

Tom shared his slippers with Tim, and together they went—clod, thump, clod, thump—upstairs.

paintbrush. Altogether it was a very unhappy quarrel, and matters might have become much worse had not Mother suddenly come on the scene and marched both boys out into the garden to cool off.

But Tim did not forget his troubles, and grizzled all the time about what Tom had done or tried to do. He told Tom that he would never let him have his paints, never.

At last they were called in to supper. And then something else went wrong.

They had to change their garden shoes and put on their slippers when they came into the house, but when they tried to do so Tim discovered that his slippers were missing. He looked high and low, but they were nowhere to be seen.

By this time Tom had his slippers on, which only made Tim more desperate.

"Huh, huh, huh," he began to grizzle again, "I can't find my slippers. Huh, huh, huh!"

Once more he looked in every corner he could think of,

wandering around in his socks crying, "Huh, huh, huh, somebody's got my slippers."

And then a beautiful thing happened.

As poor little Tim came into the dining room again crying "Huh, huh, huh" Tom took off one of his slippers and said, "Here you are, Tim; we'll have one each."

Tim's face lighted up with a smile as he eagerly seized the slipper and put it on his left foot. Then, hand in hand, they went off together to hunt for Tim's slippers. How funny it was to hear them wandering around the house—clod, thump, clod, thump, clod, thump—each with one foot in a slipper.

Suddenly there was a cry of joy. Tim's slippers had been found! In their usual place, of course, under his bed. With great rejoicing they came downstairs together, hands clasped and faces radiant.

After supper they were allowed to stay up a little while, as Mother wanted to finish the ironing before putting them to bed.

So they began painting Daddy's newspaper again, and two brushes could be seen dipping vigorously and with perfect peace and harmony into Tim's paintbox.

Tom's happy little thought had driven all the grizzles away.

# Dennis and the
# Dive Bombers

IT LOOKED AS IF all the little boys in the neighborhood were going off to war. Dennis stood at the gate of his home and watched with wide-open eager eyes as they hurried by.

Some of them carried wooden guns over their shoulders; some had wooden swords; and others had pointed sticks that were supposed to be spears.

"Where are you going?" he called to some of the boys he knew.

"Come on!" they cried excitedly. "We're going to fight the enemy."

"Who's the enemy?" asked Dennis.

"We've found a wasps' nest out in the woods, and we're all going out to do battle with them."

"Mom!" Dennis cried as he ran indoors. "May I go to war with all the other boys?"

"Whatever's this nonsense?" asked Mother.

"They're all going out to the woods to fight the wasps, and they all have swords and guns and things. Let me go too— please, Mom."

127

◄ Painting by Vernon Nye, © Review and Herald

**Two days later Dennis saw the boys going by the house again, just as they had done before, each one with his "weapon" of war.**

Just then Daddy came on the scene and asked, just as Mother had, "What's all this nonsense?" And when he heard about it, he said that Dennis was not to go under any circumstances.

"It's a very foolish errand," he said. "Wasps can be very dangerous enemies, and one must be properly prepared to fight them. You can't hope to succeed with pieces of wood. No, Dennis, you can't go."

So that was that, and Dennis had to content himself with standing at the gate waiting for the boys to come back.

After what seemed an age, the boys came rushing past, waving their weapons in the air and shouting about their great victory, although just what they had done to the wasps he never did find out.

Two days later he saw the boys going by the house again, just as they had done before, each one with his "weapon" of war.

"Come on, Dennis," they cried. "Don't be a sissy!"

"Father says I mustn't come," he said.

"Oh, come on," they called; "he won't mind. It's going to be great fun."

Dennis wavered. He could go with the boys and get back without Daddy's knowing anything about it, for he was away at his office and wouldn't be back for hours. Mom was out too. It would be such fun to go with the others, and he did so want to find out how they fought wasps with wooden swords and spears.

So picking up a piece of wood to make a weapon for himself, he sallied forth to the battle.

On reaching the woods, some of the bigger boys began searching about for a wasps' nest, and it was not long before one of them called, "I have one. Here it is. And my, aren't they big fellows!"

They *were* big fellows. Actually, they were not wasps at all but hornets, and before long *they* were going into battle,

while the poor boys were running pell-mell in every direction.

One of the hornets lit on poor Dennis, stinging him on his upper lip just under his nose. In a few moments there was a huge painful swelling.

How he wished as he hurried homeward that he had not disobeyed his daddy! What would he say? And could anything Daddy might do to him be worse than the awful pain he was suffering?

When Mother saw what had happened, she was so frightened that she took him to the doctor for treatment. Dennis suffered so much that Daddy felt he had had more than sufficient punishment. But one day when Dennis was almost better Daddy said, "Well, Dennis, so the boys didn't win that battle they went out to fight."

"No," said Dennis. "The enemy had too many dive bombers. We couldn't do a thing."

"I can think of another reason," said Daddy. "Two of them, in fact."

"What?" asked Dennis.

"First, you didn't have proper equipment—no antiaircraft guns; and second, you acted without orders."

"Maybe you're right, Daddy," said Dennis.

And of course he was.

# 23

# Tom's Thoughtlessness

SCHOOL WAS CLOSED for the afternoon and Tom was spending the free time with some of his friends in the park.

They all had brought their lunch, and after playing tag and many other games, they sat down under a fine old oak tree to enjoy the good things their mothers had packed for them.

Soon they had finished, and for want of something better to do they began throwing the banana skins and orange peels at one another and scattering their lunch papers all over the place.

All of a sudden from behind the oak tree came an elderly gentleman. He made as if to go past the boys, but stepping on one of the banana skins, he fell heavily to the ground.

Tom sprang to his side in a moment and did his best to help him to his feet again.

"I hope you're not hurt, sir," he said.

"I think not," said the gentleman. "Just a little shaken. I think I will sit on the bench for a little while if I may. I must rest a few minutes."

Tom helped him across to the bench, and the boys stood around to see whether the gentleman had hurt himself. The man sat down carefully on the bench.

"I think I'm all right," he said, "but I'm getting old now, and a fall like that is dangerous for one of my age. It's too bad that people are so careless with their banana skins, isn't it?"

"Yes," said Tom, but with a guilty look at the other boys.

"I hope you boys never throw banana skins about."

"Um," said Tom, blushing a little.

"So selfish, isn't it?" went on the elderly gentleman.

"I suppose it is," said Tom.

"If people only thought of the pain they might cause others, I'm sure they would never do it."

"No," said Tom.

"And look at all that paper lying about," said the elderly gentleman. "Some lazy, thoughtless people must have been here recently."

"Yes," said Tom, for there was really nothing else he could say.

"If only," went on the gentleman, "if only people would stop to think about others, they would never leave a mess like this behind them, would they?"

"No," said Tom, getting more uncomfortable.

"You know," said the gentleman, "this is a beautiful park, but if everyone left a mess like this, it wouldn't be worth coming to. If it were all covered with dirty paper and orange peels and banana skins you boys wouldn't want to play here, would you?"

"No, sir," said Tom and the rest together.

"Well, boys, I'm feeling better now. Thank you for helping me up. I'll be off again, I think. Here's something for you, son, to get some candy."

And so saying, to Tom's amazement, he handed him a quarter and walked away.

The boys looked at one another.

"I thought he was going to scold us," said one.

"He didn't see us," said another.

"Don't you believe it," said Tom. "I believe he saw everything we did."

"Anyhow, he was a good sport," said a third.

"And I liked what he said," said Tom. "He was very kind about it."

"You're right," said another. "And that's the last time I'm

134  going to throw stuff around here."

"I feel the same way," said Tom, and he began to pick up some of the litter he had so carelessly scattered a little while before. Strangely enough, the other boys got the same idea. They didn't say much while they were doing it, but within a few minutes all the banana skins, orange peels, and lunch papers had been picked up and dropped into one of the park trash cans.

"Well," said Tom, as he led the others off to spend the quarter, "I don't think we'll litter up this place again."

"No, we won't!" chorused the others.

And sure enough, they didn't.

STORY **24**

# Those Gooseberries

GERALD WAS FOND of gooseberries. In fact, he was so fond of them when they were nearly ripe that it was difficult for him to walk down the garden without picking one. Did I say one? I should have said several, for unless someone was looking, Gerald, I am sorry to say, would pick as many as his hands and pockets could carry.

Now it so happened that Mother also was fond of gooseberries, to say nothing of Father, who liked to walk up and down among the bushes, trying the flavor of the different berries.

One day Daddy went down the garden for a stroll, hoping to have a fat, juicy gooseberry or two when he got down to the bushes.

But when he got there, the bushes were bare. There was not a gooseberry to be seen. Even the very big one that had been growing all by itself, and which Daddy had been watching with pride and anticipation, had disappeared. The bushes had been stripped as completely as if a great wind had blown over them and swept all the gooseberries away.

"I wonder who could have taken all the gooseberries," said    135

Daddy to himself. "It surely could not have been Gerald, for I've spoken to him many times about picking them. Perhaps the birds have been at them again, or maybe Mother has picked them to make some jam."

Just then a cheery voice called to him.

"Daddy! Come and look at all the things in my garden."

It was Gerald.

Daddy walked over to the little patch he had given the boy to cultivate.

"Look, Dad, see these lovely flowers. Aren't they beautiful?"

"They surely are," said Daddy. "Nice apples you've got, too."

"Indeed they are," said Gerald. "And I hope nobody picks them but me."

"Oh, now, aren't you a bit particular about it?" said Daddy.

"I should say I am," said Gerald. "Here I've waited all the year for them, fertilized the tree and watered it and kept the weeds from it—I should think I *am* particular about who picks my apples. If Baby touches them, I'll give him a good spanking."

"I see," said Daddy, his eyes wandering over the rest of

Gerald's garden, and lighting on a pile of strange green objects lying partly concealed by a cabbage leaf.

Gerald, noticing the direction of Daddy's gaze, promptly put his foot on the cabbage leaf and began to talk about his sunflowers.

"Big sunflower that, isn't it?" he said, blushing a little.

But Daddy was not interested in sunflowers. He had become exceedingly interested in cabbages.

"Nice cabbages these," he said. "You have done well, Gerald. Do let me feel the heart of this one. You shouldn't tread on the leaves of such fine plants."

Gerald blushed more deeply as Daddy bent down to feel how solid the plant was.

"I didn't know that you had any gooseberry bushes in your garden," said Daddy rather sternly as he stood up again.

"I haven't," said Gerald very faintly and blushing more deeply.

"Then where did these skins come from?"

"Down the garden," said Gerald.

"I'm sorry," said Daddy. "I thought I could trust my boy. Don't you think it was very mean of you to take all those gooseberries when you knew how I have been waiting all year for them? Haven't you seen me down there by the hour weeding them and pruning them and fertilizing them?"

Gerald seemed to recognize his own argument and looked very sorry for himself.

"It's too bad," said Daddy. "And somehow you must learn not to do it again. Seeing you have helped yourself to my gooseberries, I think I will try a few of your apples."

So Daddy began to pick the ripest of them.

"No, no, no!" cried Gerald, bursting into tears. "You mustn't pick my apples! They're mine! I've grown them all myself!"

"But what about my gooseberries?" said Daddy, proceeding to eat the fattest and rosiest apple. "If we say six goose-

berries equal one apple, I should think I am entitled to all the
apples on this tree."

"But you mustn't pick every one of them!" cried Gerald
frantically.

"I won't, on one condition."

"What's that?" asked Gerald.

"That you promise never again to take things that do not
belong to you."

"All right. I promise," said Gerald.

"Yes," said Daddy, "and remember what the golden rule
says about doing unto others as you would like them to do
unto you."

Gerald tried hard to remember, and next year he picked his
own apples, while Daddy had
all the gooseberries he wanted.

# God's Hands

JERRY WAS WORKING in his own garden on the compound of a mission school in West Africa. Very carefully he pulled out every weed he could find. Suddenly, as he worked, he became ill. Some of his friends took him to the mission hospital.

The nurse took his temperature, put him in bed, and called the doctor.

His sickness was a great disappointment to Jerry, because it was only three weeks before the annual inspection of all the gardens by the superintendent, and he had so hoped to get the prize this year.

Every day he had worked his hardest, digging, planting, weeding, and striving his utmost to make his the best garden at the mission. But now all his hopes seemed shattered.

As he lay in the hospital he pictured the weeds growing up—they grow very quickly in West Africa—and spoiling all he had done. As inspection day drew nearer and he was not allowed to get up, he knew there was no possible hope of his winning. The other boys would be working hard on their gardens and making them look all spick and span. He didn't stand a chance.

Meanwhile something was happening at the mission. Daniel, Jerry's friend, had a bright idea. He, too, was going in for the competition, but he thought it was too bad that

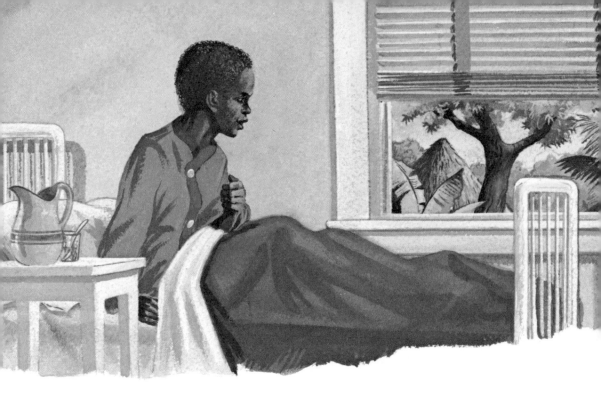

Jerry should stand no chance at all because of his illness. He had talked to the other boys about it, and they had all agreed to give just a little time each day to keeping the weeds out of Jerry's garden until inspection day came around. So while they still tried to make their own gardens the best, they gave a little extra care and love to that of the poor sick boy who could not look after his own.

At last inspection day arrived. Jerry was still lying in the hospital, and he was discouraged. He thought he could see his garden covered with weeds. He pictured the superintendent going around and saying, "Whose garden is that with all those dreadful weeds in it?" Then he seemed to hear some of the boys saying, "Oh, that's Jerry's garden."

It was too bad, he thought, that it should happen like this after all my work—and he knew he had worked harder than the others. But there was nothing he could do about it now.

Jerry was becoming more and more miserable when the door of the ward opened, and to his surprise in walked the su-

"We have come to congratulate you," said the superintendent, "on winning the prize for the best-kept garden this year."

"Me?" said Jerry, with eyes wide open.

"Yes, you," said the superintendent.

"But—but—it's all covered with weeds."

"It wasn't when I saw it this morning," said the superintendent.

"But—how—what——?" began Jerry.

"It's all right," said Daniel with a twinkle in his eye. "We are all happy that you have won the prize. You see, God didn't let the weeds grow in your garden because you deserved to win; He knew you had worked harder than us all."

"I think that's right," said the superintendent; "but I believe He had some human hands to help Him."

At this all the boys laughed happily and ran out again to their work, while Jerry, overjoyed, dropped a little tear of gladness on his pillow.

STORY **26**

# Daddy's
# Discovery

RONALD RETURNED FROM SCHOOL one day looking sick. As he came indoors he walked across the dining room and flopped into an armchair.

"What's the matter, Ronny?" asked Mother. "You don't look very well."

"Don't feel well," said Ronald.

"What have you been eating at school today?" asked Mother.

"Haven't eaten anything since dinner," said Ronny. "I just feel sick. Don't worry. I'll be better tomorrow."

"Well, supper is nearly ready."

"Don't want any supper."

"What do you want?"

"Oh, nothing. I don't need any supper or anything. I think I'll go to bed early."

"Daddy will be back at seven; better wait till then; he likes to find you here."

"No," said Ronald, "I'm going now. Right away." So saying he went upstairs, and from the noises overhead Mother guessed that he was getting undressed right away, and that he wasn't wasting any time about it.

At seven Daddy came in. "Where's Ronald?" he asked.

"In bed," said Mother.

"In bed!" repeated Daddy with surprise. "What for? I'll go up and see him."

Daddy bounded upstairs and into Ronald's room.

"What's the matter, son?" he asked.

Ronald pretended to be asleep, but Daddy knew a thing or two about that, having tried the same trick himself sometimes when he was a little boy.

"Come on now, Ronny. You're not asleep. What's the matter?"

"Feeling sick," murmured Ronny.

"Give me your hand. Let me feel your pulse."

Ronny held out his hand. Daddy felt his pulse and noticed something.

"What's this on your fingers, son?"

Ronny pulled his hand under the covers. "Nothing, Dad; paint, I think."

"Let me see your tongue."

Ronald opened his mouth. Daddy bent down very close, much closer than he really needed just to look in. Then he got up from the bed and walked over to the chair where Ronald's

clothes were lying. He picked them up one by one and felt carefully in the pockets. That was a messy job, for some of the pockets had all sorts of treasures in them, such as bits of string, nails, dirty handkerchiefs, a half-melted caramel, an apple core, and cooky crumbs. But from the bottom of the right-hand trouser pocket Daddy hauled out a small yellow box.

He came back to Ronny, who had been lying very quiet and still during the search.

"Ronny, why do you have these matches in your pocket?"

"To light fireworks," said Ronny quietly.

"Are you sure, Ronny?" said Daddy very solemnly. "Are you really telling me the truth?"

There was a long silence.

"Tell me," said Daddy, "was that the truth?"

"No," said Ronald very, very quietly.

"I knew it wasn't," said Daddy. "As soon as I saw your hand and smelled your breath I knew you had been playing with tobacco. Am I right?"

"Yes; a boy at school dared me to try it," said Ronald, tears streaming down his cheeks.

"Oh, Ronny! I am so sorry," said Daddy. "I had hoped you would never learn that horrid, dirty, wasteful habit. I have never smoked tobacco in my life, and I wanted my son never, never to have anything to do with it."

"I knew you didn't, Daddy, and I really didn't want to," said Ronny amid his tears.

"I'm sure you didn't," said Daddy. "But you must be strong next time to say No. Smoking never did anybody any good. It spoils your health, weakens your heart and lungs, stains your hands, makes your breath smell, and burns up your money. Not only that, but young people who get hooked on tobacco often go on to use even stronger drugs. Then the result may be broken health, a ruined mind, prison, or even death."

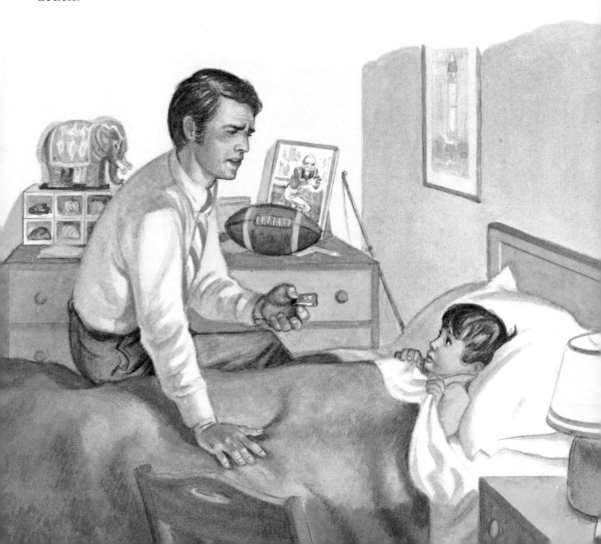

Daddy paused, and there was a deep silence, broken only
by Ronny's deep breathing and an occasional sob.

"Ronny!" said Daddy.

"Yes, Daddy."

"I hope you'll promise me one thing."

"Yes, Daddy."

"Give me your hand."

Ronny put it out. "Promise me," said Daddy, taking
Ronny's hand in his, "promise me that you will never put tobacco of any kind in your mouth again."

"I promise," said Ronny.

They squeezed hands warmly in confidence, and the
promise was sealed.

STORY **27**

# How Toby
# Made Peace

"NOW LOOK HERE, CHILDREN," said
Daddy, sending Paul and Barbara out of the living room into
the garden. "I simply can't stand it any longer. You stay outside until you can learn to stop grumbling and be more po-
lite."

And with that Daddy went back into the living room, sat
down in his easy chair, put his feet up on the footstool, and
went to sleep.

Paul and Barbara knew they deserved their fate, and soon
began to feel sorry that their behavior had annoyed Daddy so
much.

For a little while they did not know what to do, and wandered aimlessly up and down the garden path in silence.

"Ah, here's Toby coming!" cried Paul. "Toby, Toby, Toby!
Good old Toby, where have you been?"

Toby wagged his tail, as if to assure them that he had
been a very good dog indeed all the time he had been missing.

"And you haven't been chasing any cats?" asked Barbara.
Toby merely yawned, then wagged his tail again, as if to say

149

that he wouldn't think of doing any such thing, although, if the truth must be told, there was nothing that so stirred Toby's wrath as the sight of a kitty's whiskers.

"I've got an idea," said Paul.

"Tell me," said Barbara.

"Let's give Toby a bath; he hasn't had one for a long time, and he's getting quite dirty."

"I think that would be fun," said Barbara. "It's better than doing nothing. You get the tub out of the shed, and I'll slip into the kitchen quietly and see if I can find a towel and some soap."

"Right!" cried Paul. "And won't that be nice, Toby? Toby have a bath? Dear old Toby!"

Again Toby wagged his tail, though it was not quite so happy a wag as before. He was not fond of being bathed, and sometimes objected to it very strongly. He looked suspiciously at the tub as Paul brought it out of the shed, and decided it was about time he took a short walk down the garden.

Barbara soon returned, bringing a towel and a kettle of warm water.

"Where's Toby?" she asked.

"Ran off," said Paul. "We'll have to catch him."

"Toby, Toby!" called Barbara.

But Toby was a wise old dog and guessed why he was wanted. He walked a little farther on. Paul and Barbara followed him, and after an exciting chase caught him in a corner by the greenhouse.

"Bad Tody! Bad Toby!" said Paul as he dragged him by the collar up toward the shed. "Toby mustn't run away from us anymore. Toby's going to have a nice bath."

Toby didn't appreciate the last remark at all. His tail had stopped wagging and his eyes had a strange, determined look.

It was quite a job to get him into the tub. Paul lifted his

front legs and Barbara his back legs, and together they got
him in. But it was quite another matter to keep him in. For a
moment or two he stood quite still while Paul sponged his
ears. Then all of a sudden he began to kick and jump and
splash water all over.

"Hold him, Paul," cried Barbara, "or he'll jump out of the
tub!"

"Can't you see I'm holding him as hard as I can?" said
Paul. "You go on washing him."

Barbara began to wash him while Paul tried his best to
keep Toby in the tub. She got as far as covering the whole of
him with a good lather of soap, when suddenly something
happened.

For a moment Toby became very still. He seemed to forget
that he was being bathed. His eyes had caught sight of something down in the garden. His back stiffened, his tail stood
up, and with a loud "Yap, yap" he shook his collar free,

leaped from the tub, and dashed away at top speed.

"Stop him!" cried Barbara helplessly, wiping the water from her dress and ankles.

"You'll never stop him!" said Paul. "Can't you see there's Mrs. Tompkins' cat!"

"Oh dear!" cried Barbara. "I do hope he doesn't hurt her."

There was no fear of that, for this particular kitty had often been chased by Toby, and knew every possible hiding place in both the garden and the house.

"Oh, look!" cried Barbara, as dog and cat raced back and forth, across the flower beds, in and out among the trees and bushes. "What a dreadful mess Toby will be!"

She was right. By this time Toby's soap-covered body had gathered up mud, leaves, and bits of twigs, until he looked as if he'd never had a bath in his life.

"I only hope Daddy doesn't look out the window until we've got the little rascal cleaned up," said Paul.

"You're right," said Barbara.

But there was no need for them to worry about Daddy; he

was still sleeping soundly, quite unconscious of what was
going on outside.

"Now you can catch him," said Barbara as kitty made a sudden turn and came rushing up the garden toward them, Toby close behind. "Grab him as he goes by."

But it was easier said than done. Paul made a grab, but his hand got only a greasy mixture of soap and mud, and away went Toby faster than ever.

"Look!" cried Barbara. "Look where the cat's going."

Growing tired and seeking a place of safety, kitty had spied the half-open window of the living room.

With a mighty spring she leaped onto the window sill, dropped down inside, and dived under an armchair that was drawn up near the fireplace.

Paul and Barbara held their breath. Would Toby follow? Could he possibly jump so high?

"Toby! Toby!" they both shrieked, hoping to call him away.

It was in vain. With a jump such as he had never made before, Toby got his paws up on the window sill and scrambled over. He was in the living room. Dirty, muddy, soapy Toby was in the living room!

All that happened next had better not be printed. Suffice it to say that Toby, forgetting the object of his chase in the presence of his master, jumped up in his usual friendly way upon the sleeping form in the armchair. Waking with a start, Daddy found his hands clasping a strange, warm, wriggling, soapy mass upon his knees.

154 "What *shall* we do?" said Paul. "Daddy will be awfully cross with us."

"There's only one thing to do," said Barbara. "We had better go in right now and say we're sorry."

"All right," said Paul. "I'll come with you."

And away they went. As they reached the living room, the French doors opened and out came Toby, a little more quickly even than he had gone in. Daddy stood inside. He looked very stern. As for his clothes, they were a terrible sight. Simply covered with soapy dirt!

"We are dreadfully sorry," said Barbara. "We never dreamed he would do it, and we'll clean up all the mess and brush your trousers and everything. Please forgive us."

Daddy looked at the two children and then down at his clothes. Then his face broke into the least bit of a smile.

"Oh, you two terrible children!" he said. "But I suppose I shall have to forgive you once again."

And Paul and Barbara put their arms around his neck and hugged him ever so tight.

# 28

# Unlucky Jim

JIM THOUGHT HE WAS the most unlucky boy who had ever been born. Everything seemed to go wrong with him. Life looked particularly dark for him just now, for only a few minutes ago his one and only glass marble had rolled down a drain.

But quite apart from this, he had much to make him feel blue. For one thing, he was shivering with cold. He should have had warm stockings and underclothes to wear, but he hadn't any, because there was not enough money to buy them. Father was out of work.

For another thing, he was hungry. It was some hours since lunch, and the bread and butter he'd had then seemed to have gone clear down to the South Pole. As he trudged along the streets with his hands in his pockets, he saw lots of other boys and girls going into beautiful homes for their supper, and he knew that he would have to climb up the dirty, narrow stairs of a dingy, crowded apartment for the little bit of bread and jam he would get.

Just then he passed a toyshop all ablaze with lights and full of everything that might make a boy's heart glad. He   155

stopped a moment and watched other boys and girls coming out with brown paper packages under their arms. He jabbed his hand a little deeper down into his pocket and fingered his nickel once again, his very last coin. How he wished that he could buy something to take to his little sister, lying at home so sick—something she would really like.

"If I ain't the unluckiest fellow that ever lived!" he said to himself.

But the next day his luck changed. He was walking down the street when a well-dressed woman stopped and spoke to him.

"Is your name Jimmie Mackay?" she asked.

"Yes, ma'am," said Jimmie, surprised, and wondering what was going to happen.

"Well," said the woman, "we have your name on a list at our church, and we want you to come to a special Christmas party next week. Here is a ticket for you."

"Oh, my!" said Jimmie, not knowing what else to say. "But what about Jean—she's my sister, y' know; she'll be better by then, perhaps; she ought to come too."

"I'm afraid we can take only one from each family this time," said the woman kindly. "We will try to take Jean next time."

"Well, that's lucky and unlucky," said Jim to himself as

the woman walked away. "Lucky for me and unlucky for poor Jean."

Then a bright idea occurred to him—perhaps he could let Jean go instead of him. He looked at his card. It read "Admit bearer—Jimmie Mackay—only."

"Unlucky again!" murmured Jimmie.

So Jimmie went to the party. For the greater part of the time he forgot all about his troubles. Everything was so different, so very wonderful. He had never, never had so much to eat.

After the meal they all played games until it was time for the presents on the Christmas tree to be given away. What excitement there was then, especially as each child was to be allowed to choose just what he wanted most.

Jim could hardly sit still as he watched the other children going up in front of him. He felt as if he were on pins and needles. He had seen such a wonderful toy fire engine hanging on the tree—something he had wanted all his life; and how he did hope and hope and *hope* that no one else would ask for it first!

At last—after what seemed hours—Jimmie's turn came to make his choice.

"Jimmie Mackay!" called out the woman by the tree.

Jimmie jumped from his seat like a shell from a cannon. All he could see was the red fire truck. It was still there!

As he approached the woman he noticed that she was the very one who had spoken to him in the street and given him his ticket for the party. Immediately a new idea entered his mind.

"And what would you like to have, Jimmie?" asked the woman. "You may have any one thing you like from the tree."

What an offer! Jimmie could scarcely take it in. He stood and gazed up at the sparkling, heavily laden tree. Once more his eye caught sight of the fire truck.

Painting by Manning De V. Lee, © Review and Heral

**"Most of all," Jimmie said, "I would like tha red engine; but if you don't mind, I will tak that doll over there."**

"Most of all," he said, looking up at the lady, "I would like that red fire truck; but if you don't mind, I will take that doll over there."

Tears filled his eyes as he said it, but with great resolution he kept his face straight.

Somehow the woman seemed to understand, and without a word she brought Jimmie the doll. As he went away, she squeezed his hand, and, bending down, whispered, "God bless you, Jimmie."

But the other children did not understand at all. There were giggles and snickers, then whoops and yells as they told the world that Jimmie had chosen a doll! Some of the boys called out, "Sissy!" and others, with a laugh, "Imagine a boy taking a doll!" And the little girls said, "That was just the doll we wanted!"

Jimmie blushed. He couldn't help it. Finally he became so uncomfortable that he put on his cap and went out, with the doll under his arm.

All the way home he thought about the bad luck that seemed to have dogged his footsteps. First, he had lost his fire truck, and second, he had been laughed at by the whole crowd of children.

"If I'm not the unluckiest fellow——" he began. Then he felt the doll under his arm. At once his thoughts brightened and his step quickened.

A few minutes later he was up in the little dark bedroom where Jean lay sick in bed.

"I'm so glad you've come!" said Jean. "It's so lonely here all by myself. And what have you got there?" she asked, sitting up in bed and peering at the doll with eager eyes. "Is that for me? Oh, Jimmie, Jimmie, you *are* a dear!"

Jimmie forgot all about his bad luck. A thrill of joy went through him as he saw his sister's delight.

Just then there was a knock at the door. It was the woman from the church. "What——" began Jimmie.

"I've come to say how sorry I am that the children were 161 so unkind to you this evening," interrupted the woman. "They are sorry too, now. I told them why you chose the doll. And they asked me to bring you something for yourself. Here it is. Now I must go, for it is getting late. Good night!" and she was gone.

Jimmie gasped, and then opened the package.

It was the fire engine!

Then he danced a jig around Jean's bed, chuckling to himself, and saying, "If I'm not the luckiest fellow alive!"

STORY **29**

# Sticking Pins Into Billy

WILLIAM ARNOLD CROKER, known to the other boys in the town as "Billy," was a bright lad, but he had one fault. He thought so much of himself that his hat would hardly go on his head.

Billy's skill in games made him a natural leader of the boys, but they all secretly disliked him because he was always bragging about the wonderful things he could do. He never had time to listen to what the other boys had to say, but would always interrupt them with an account of some experience he had had. If someone said he had seen a big frog, Billy would say, "That's nothing; last week I saw a frog much bigger than that."

At last the other boys became tired of his boasting, and began to talk over ways and means of putting an end to it. As Tommy Walters said, Billy was swollen up with pride as big as a balloon, and it was high time somebody stuck a nice big pin into him.

But how to do it was another question. Some of the boys suggested ducking him in the river; but Billy was quite a strong boy, and none of the others wanted to take the risk of

162

a personal quarrel with him. Then Tommy struck on a bright idea.

"I know of something better than that," he said. "It wouldn't be kind to put him in the river, and it wouldn't do him much good anyhow. Have you ever thought what is the matter with Billy?"

The others crowded around. "No, what?" they asked. They were in a mood to try anything.

"I'll tell you. You've all noticed how Billy seems to win all our games," said Tommy. "That's the trouble with him; he thinks we're no good, and that he can always beat us. I'm tired of his superior airs. If we are going to stop his bragging, we must learn to play better ourselves."

"Pretty good sense," said another boy. "If we could make Billy lose every game for a few weeks, he would soon change his tune."

"You're right," said Tommy, "but it's up to us to beat him. Why not practice some of our games on the quiet, and surprise Billy?"

"But we can't all win," said a pale-faced, timid youngster;

"and I don't see how we can practice all the games we play."

"Of course we can't all practice everything at once," said Tommy. "No; but let one or two practice running, some jumping, and others marbles. I'm going to practice so I can throw him out at first base the next time we play."

"Great!" laughed the others. "Let's do it."

Tommy's idea certainly did put new life into those boys. Their mothers and teachers soon began to wonder what was the matter with them, for nearly all of them began to practice hard at the games they had chosen in their secret meeting.

Billy, too, noticed it but did not suspect that all this effort was directed against him. As the days went by, he began to notice the results of the plan. In running races he had always been able to keep an easy lead, but a few of the boys now began to keep up with him, and some passed him. Instead of always winning, he learned what it means to lose.

When the school field day came around, so many pins were stuck into Billy that he was reduced to almost normal size. Billy had not bothered to practice for any of the events because he felt so certain of success. The other boys, however,

had worked very hard with but one purpose in view, and they
won. Poor Billy did not win a single race.

He felt very bad about it, but was sure he would be able to regain his lost reputation at the baseball game that was to follow the field events, for he prided himself on being a very good hitter.

This ball game was always a big affair, at least in the boys' eyes, for it was held on the town diamond, and usually there were many spectators.

Billy was up first. He told the boys that he was going to make at least ten runs, and that they had better keep their eye on the town clock, for he was going to hit a ball right in the middle of it. Then, carrying his bat with a real swagger, he strolled across the field as if he were a professional. But much to his surprise, Billy fanned out.

In the next inning Tommy was up first. He saw at once that his great opportunity had come. After all he had said to the other boys, he knew what he must do.

Tommy had been practicing batting and fielding every morning and evening. In the morning, before his fa-

ther went to work, Tommy would get him out into the vacant lot next to the house to pitch him a few balls. After school he would get one of the boys to play with him. Then in the evening after supper his father would throw him a few more, until his eye and timing were nearly perfect, and he could hit curves as hard as straight balls. So now he really felt ready for the big game.

Tommy walked out to the batter's box with more assurance than ever before. The pitcher shot him a fast ball. But Tommy was ready; he had been training his eye carefully, and he was sure of his swing. To the surprise of all, he hit the ball away out, and before the left fielder recovered the ball, Tommy was rounding third. The left fielder threw to Billy, who was catching, but Billy dropped the ball, and Tommy slid in home—a home run.

Tommy made two more home runs that day, one in the last inning with two out and two men on base, partly because Billy, who was really a good player, lost his nerve at being

surpassed, and partly because he worked so hard to succeed. Billy failed to make a single run in the game.

At the close of the game they all crowded around Tommy and proclaimed him hero of the day.

As for Billy, no one would have thought he was the same boy who had walked so confidently onto the diamond a couple of hours before.

"How about the town clock?" piped a small voice.

"And how about those ten runs?" ventured a bolder voice among the boys.

But Billy only walked away with his head down. That was the last "pin" that Billy needed to have stuck into him. No one ever heard him boasting again.

# Four Jars
# of Jam

TUBBY AND TOBY had just returned home from the big city. They were very much excited and very tired, though they wouldn't admit it, for they had spent the whole day with Mother walking around a wonderful exhibition. It had been such fun! They had seen so many interesting things that when they began to tell Daddy about them they got all mixed up.

Then they began to bring out the treasures they had gathered during the day. Both of them had a collection of the most delightful little samples you could wish to see—tiny pieces of cheese wrapped in silver paper, packages of cookies and cornflakes, and, best of all, four dainty little jars of jam.

Oh, those jars of jam! What shrieks of delight greeted their unpacking! How pretty they looked, standing on the table with the light shining through them. One was strawberry jam, one apricot jam, one black currant jelly, and the other marmalade. Tubby and Toby took quite a long time to decide how the four jars should be divided, but at last Tubby agreed to have the strawberry and the apricot, and Toby took the black currant jelly and the marmalade.

Fancy having two whole jars of jam each! It seemed too wonderful to be true. Tubby and Toby stood them up beside their plates at suppertime so they could keep their eyes on them. Of course, they were not very big jars, but to the happy, excited eyes of Tubby and Toby they were more precious than the biggest jars in Mother's cupboard.

All through suppertime they talked about these four treasured jam jars—how they got them, and what they were going to do with them. They were quite sure they were going to eat all the jam themselves, and that if they tasted only a spoonful every day the jars would last for weeks and weeks.

Supper was almost over when Daddy said something that upset things a bit.

"Poor old Dad!" he said, talking as though to himself in a very disconsolate tone of voice. "Poor old Dad! He never has a jam jar all to himself. Nobody ever gives him anything. Poor old Dad!"

Tubby and Toby stopped talking. They both looked at Daddy in surprise, questioning in their minds whether he really meant what he said. Then they looked at their precious jam jars.

"Here, Daddy," said Tubby, "have my jar of strawberry jam."

"You darling boy!" said Daddy. "I don't want to take your jam. It was only fun."

"But you must have it," said Tubby, setting the jar of strawberry jam down with a bang in front of Daddy's plate. "You see, I still have the apricot left."

Daddy nearly shed a tear at this, but he didn't because he was too busy watching Toby out of the corner of his eye.

The struggle was harder for Toby. He was breathing deeply and looking hard at one jar and then at the other. He picked up the marmalade, put it down, then picked up the black currant jelly. His solemn little face showed that a big battle was being fought inside.

"Daddy," he said at last, "I think I will let you have one of mine as well. You can have this jar of black currant jelly."

And with that Toby plumped the jar of black currant jelly down beside Daddy's plate.

"You dear, precious boys," said Daddy. "Of course I won't eat your lovely jam; but I am pleased you gave it to me. I'll remember it forever and ever."

# Harry's Motorboat

THE GREAT DREAM of Harry's life had come true. For years and years, so it seemed, Harry had longed for a real motorboat, one that would go all by itself without having to be wound up; and now at last it had come. Only this morning his uncle had brought him one as a birthday present.

What happiness!

First of all, of course, it had to be tried in the bathtub, just to see whether it really would go. But after Harry had seen it get up steam and go up and down the tub a score of times he could not rest until he had taken it to the lake.

So, carefully holding his precious little power boat he proudly started off toward the lake.

"You *will* be careful, won't you?" said Mother.

"Of course," promised Harry.

"And be sure to be back by six o'clock?"

"Yes, Mother."

And away he went.

What fun he did have! What a thrill it was to put his boat into the water and start the motor.

Away went the little boat across the lake, while Harry rushed round in his bare feet to meet it at the other side. So excited was he that he walked into the water to meet it coming in. Turning it round, he sent it off again, this time toward a different spot.

Time goes quickly when one is happy, and Harry did not notice how the hours were slipping by. At last, however, lengthening shadows aroused him, and he stopped a passerby to ask him the time.

"Half past five."

"Phew!" whistled Harry. "I'll have to be packing up soon. Just time for one more trip."

But how often it happens that the one more is really one too many!

Anyway, so it happened with poor Harry. For the last trip he decided to send the boat the longest possible journey. If it reached the point aimed at, he thought, it would be quite near to the footpath that led toward home. So, he argued, it would really save time if he made the last trip the longest.

Away went the motorboat on her "transatlantic" crossing, with Harry's delighted eyes following her every inch of the way.

"She's halfway across!" he muttered to himself.

Then his heart seemed to stand still. The boat had stopped. What happened, he could not tell. Perhaps he had used the boat too much for one afternoon; perhaps it needed oil; perhaps, dreadful thought, it had caught in some reeds. Poor Harry did not know. He stood there on the bank with eyes glued on the boat, hoping against hope that it would start again. But it did not move. That it had caught on something he became convinced. How could he get it back? Far in the distance he heard a factory whistle.

"That's the five-to-six whistle," he said to himself, "and I must be home at six!"

Poor Harry! What should he do? He *must* keep his promise

◀ Painting by Vernon Nye

**What a thrill it was to put his boat into the water and watch it glide away.**

to his mother, for he always did, but if he went away, someone would be sure to get the boat before he could return. In
desperation he walked into the water as far as he dared go,
but he found that it suddenly became very deep just a few
yards from the shore and he had to return.

Again he looked at the little boat quietly bobbing up and
down in the middle of the lake. Then he thought of the time.

"Oh, what shall I do?" he said to himself.

There was no one about to whom he could turn for help,
for the few who had been there in the afternoon had already
gone home. Suddenly an unusual thought came into his
mind. Some of you may smile when I tell you what it was. It
was the music of a hymn he had sung in church a few days
before. Presently the words came back to him.

> "What a friend we have in Jesus,
> All our sins and griefs to bear;
> What a privilege to carry
> Everything to God in prayer."

"But," Harry said to himself, "surely Jesus isn't interested in my little motorboat!" He almost smiled at the thought. Then in his desperate anxiety he said, "Why not? Perhaps He is."

And right there by the lake side Harry shut his eyes for just a second and asked Jesus to look after his little boat while he ran home to keep his promise to his mother.

Taking one last, loving look at his precious boat, he turned away and ran home as fast as he could go.

He was a few minutes late, but Mother said nothing about it, for she saw at once that he was very upset. When she learned that he had even left his boat behind in the lake in order to keep his promise to her she felt very proud of him indeed.

"After supper," she said, "we will both go back, even though it is dark, and see what we can do with a ball of string."

Supper did not take long, I can assure you, and by half past seven Harry and his mother were on their way back to the lake, with a flashlight and string enough to stretch across.

By the time they arrived, a pale moon was rising, casting its rays across the silent waters.

Eagerly they both strained their eyes, hoping to catch a glimpse of the little boat.

"It was over there," said Harry, "right in the middle."

"I can't see it," said Mother.

"Neither can I," said Harry with a trace of fear in his voice.

"Perhaps when the moon gets up a bit——" began Mother with a note of encouragement.

"No," said Harry disconsolately, "it's gone. I know just where it was. It must have sunk."

They walked all around the lake, hoping by chance it might have drifted ashore. But nowhere was there a trace of it.

"There's no use looking anymore," sighed Harry. "Let's go home."

And in his heart he said, "And what was the good of asking Jesus to look after it?"

Crunch! Heavy footsteps nearby startled them both. "Hello!" called a deep voice. "What are you doing here in the dark?"

It was the game warden.

"I lost my motorboat this afternoon," said Harry, "and

Mother and I have come down to look for it."

"Have you found it?" asked the man more kindly.

"No, we haven't," said Harry.

"Shouldn't think you had," he said, "in the dark. It's late now. You'd better follow me."

Something in his tone of voice raised Harry's hopes.

They turned and followed the man along the lake shore. Presently they reached an old boathouse. The game warden stopped, pulled out a bunch of keys, and opened the creaky door.

"Bring your flashlight over here," he said.

As Mother held it, the beam fell on the precious motorboat!

"There it is, there it is!" cried Harry. "How did you get it out of the lake?"

"With my boat," said the game warden. "I saw it caught in the reeds and guessed some boy would be looking for it. So I just rowed out and brought it in."

"Thank you ever so much!" said Harry as he and Mother said good night to the game warden. Then they hurried homeward, Harry gripping the motorboat as though there were danger of his losing it again.

And on the way his heart sent up a silent thanksgiving to the Friend who never forgets a request, and who even answers the prayer of a boy for his boat.

STORY **32**

# A Little Child
# Shall Lead Them

YOU MAY THINK this is a made-up story, but it isn't. It is absolutely true. I know the little boy and girl it concerns very well indeed, and it was their mother who told it to me.

Of course the names are not real. I couldn't tell you the real names, could I? So I will call the boy Donald and the girl Margaret. Margaret was five, and Donald eight and a half.

It so happened that one day when Mother was clearing up the dining room she threw an old Christmas card on the fire. It was a very old one that had been sent to Margaret at least four years before.

Hardly was it alight, however, when Margaret began to make a fuss.

"That's my Christmas card," she cried. "You shouldn't have burned it. I've kept it all this time, and I want it."

"But it was such a dirty card," said Mother, trying to make the matter right. "And it has been lying about the place for such a long time I thought you didn't want it any-more."

"But of course I wanted it!" cried Margaret, getting more angry. "You should have known I wanted it. Why should you burn my things, anyway?"

Mother tried calmly to explain to Margaret that she had lots of other cards, that all together they were of no real value, and that very soon there would be another Christmas, when her friends probably would be sending her many more.

But Margaret refused to be reasoned with, and began calling her mother some very unkind names. Whereupon Mother tried another method of helping her little daughter —and the neighbors must have wondered what was happening next door. Just what happened I will leave you to guess, but I can tell you that very shortly afterward a sobbing little girl was getting in between a pair of sheets upstairs.

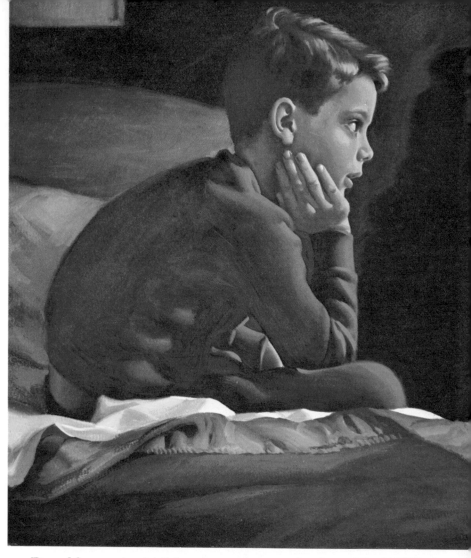

Donald was in bed by now also, and when Mother had kissed them both good night and gone out of the room, he began to talk to his little sister. Mother, on the stairs, stopped to listen.

"Margaret," said Donald, "you must be a good girl and go to sleep."

"I can't go to sleep," said Margaret. "I've been so bad, and I don't want Mother to spank me anymore."

"Yes, dear," said Donald, with sympathy and wisdom beyond his years, "you have been very bad, and it made me

feel so sad and ill inside, but if you would just say a little prayer all for yourself, it would make everything all right."

"But I don't know what to say," said Margaret, amid the tears and sobs that shook her little body.

"If you like, Margaret, I will help you," said Donald, "and you could say it after me. Shall I?"

"Yes, please."

There was a pause. Then Donald began:

"Dear Lord Jesus. Now, Margaret, say it after me."

Painting by Russell Harlan

**"If you say a little prayer, Jesus will forgive your naughtiness," said Donald. "But I don't know what to say," Margaret sobbed.**

182     "Dear Lord Jesus," repeated Margaret.

"Help me not to be bad," said Donald.

"Help me not to be bad," repeated Margaret.

"Forgive me for showing so much temper tonight."

The sobs increased, and for a while Margaret did not speak.

At last she repeated, "Forgive me for showing so much temper tonight."

"And make me a good little girl," continued Donald.

"And make me a good little girl," repeated Margaret.

"And please wash all my sins away, for Jesus Christ's sake. Amen," said Donald.

Margaret again repeated after him.

"Is that all now, Donald?" she asked.

"Yes, dear," said Donald; "don't cry anymore now. You know, the sheet you've spoiled in your book in heaven—where the angels write all that we do—has now been smudged all over with something like red, *ever so red*, crayon, and it has hidden all the writing about your naughty tricks, and no one can ever read about them again. That's just what Jesus does when we are sorry and ask Him to forgive us. Aren't you happy, Margaret?"

"Oh, yes, Donald. I feel better now. And Mother won't spank me anymore?"

"No, Margaret, 'course not. You've asked Jesus to make you good, and if we're good, Mom and Dad are happy, and then they never have to spank us, do they?"

"No," said Margaret.

"Good night," said Donald.

"Good night, Donald," said Margaret. "I'm so glad it's all right now."

Then silence, while Mother crept softly downstairs with tears in her eyes and gladness in her heart, happy to know that her darlings had already found a friend in Jesus, and were learning so soon to roll their burden upon the Lord.

STORY **33**

# Three Wonderful Songs

HOW BETTER COULD WE CLOSE this book than with a story of angel songs?

Are you quite still and very quiet? I hope so, for I want you to hear these songs in all their glory.

Now let your thoughts wander back over the years, back and back and back, before you were born, before Daddy was born, before Grandma was born, before there were any cars or buses or houses or churches—yes, before there were any cats or dogs or horses, even before there were any flowers or trees. And now, amid the silence and the darkness, let us stand still in reverence and watch God making the world.

Suddenly a Voice, majestic and musical, rings through the realms of space: "Let there be light!" The darkness vanishes, and light breaks over the waste of waters. Again the Voice is heard, and the sky is made, and the dry land rises from the waters, grass grows upon the mountains and the valleys, and the trees spring up—apple trees, plum trees, pear trees, and all the beautiful trees in the woods. Again and again the Voice is heard; the fishes appear in the sea, the birds fly in the air, and the animals are created upon the

183

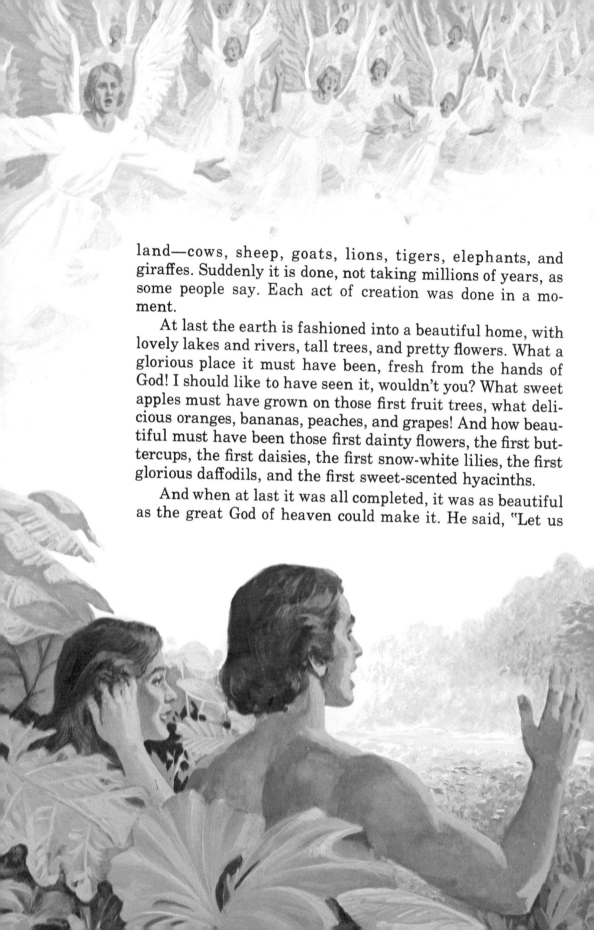

land—cows, sheep, goats, lions, tigers, elephants, and giraffes. Suddenly it is done, not taking millions of years, as some people say. Each act of creation was done in a moment.

At last the earth is fashioned into a beautiful home, with lovely lakes and rivers, tall trees, and pretty flowers. What a glorious place it must have been, fresh from the hands of God! I should like to have seen it, wouldn't you? What sweet apples must have grown on those first fruit trees, what delicious oranges, bananas, peaches, and grapes! And how beautiful must have been those first dainty flowers, the first buttercups, the first daisies, the first snow-white lilies, the first glorious daffodils, and the first sweet-scented hyacinths.

And when at last it was all completed, it was as beautiful as the great God of heaven could make it. He said, "Let us make man in our image, after our likeness." Then from the dust of the ground, with His wonderful creative power, God formed the first man and the first woman, the father and mother of all the people in the world. He did not make them first as monkeys, as some people say, and let them grow into men. That is a mistake made by people who doubt the creation story. No, the Bible tells us "God created man in his own image, in the image of God he created him" (Genesis 1:27, R.S.V.).

And then, suddenly, as the living man and woman stood on their feet, tall and beautiful, and looked out with happy, eager eyes upon the wonderful home that God had made for them, all heaven burst into song. With great eagerness the angels had watched each step in the process of creation, and now, in this supreme moment, they broke into a chorus of adoring praise to God. " 'The morning stars sang together, and all the sons of God shouted for joy' " (Job 38:7, R.S.V.).

Can you hear them singing? How the mighty sound surges through the sky and rolls around the clouds! Rising and falling as the wind wafts the melody here and there, it grows stronger and deeper and richer as it sweeps to its climax and they sing: " 'Holy, holy, holy is the Lord of hosts; the whole earth is full of his glory' " (Isaiah 6:3, R.S.V.).

How long the angels sang I do not know, but I am sure that when at last Adam and Eve did wrong, and sin came in to spoil their beautiful home, they must have wept in disappointment. And as they saw the people of the world become more and more wicked and disobedient as the years passed by, their sorrow must have been deep indeed. There was no more rejoicing in heaven, and their only comfort was found in the promise that one day their beloved Leader would go down to earth, and in some way recover what had been lost, and turn men's hearts back to God.

The next wonderful song was sung at the birth of Jesus, a very long time afterward. Did it seem long to the angels? Perhaps. Anyhow, many times they must have wondered just how and when the promise was going to be fulfilled. At last the great hour for which they had yearned and waited so long arrived. To their amazement and wonder they saw their Leader go down to the world, not in power and glory but as a little baby, to grow up as a boy among boys, as a man among men. They could not understand it, but they were confident that His way must be best.

Eagerly they followed every detail of the plan. Then one night they gathered around Bethlehem in tens of thousands, and when the wonderful news flashed to the waiting angels that Jesus at last was born, their hearts thrilled with joy. They had to tell somebody; so they appeared to shepherds in the field, the only people who were awake at the time.

" 'Be not afraid,' " said Gabriel; " 'for behold, I bring you good news of a great joy which will come to all the people; for to you is born this day in the city of David a Savior, who is Christ the Lord' " (Luke 2:10, 11, R.S.V.).

And then upon the eyes of the astonished shepherds burst the glorious vision of the heavenly host, and upon their ears fell angelic music such as no mortal had ever heard.

" 'Glory to God in the highest, and on earth peace among men' " (verse 14, R.S.V.).

◄ Painting by B. Plockhorst

Upon the ears of the shepherds fell the strains of angels singing, "Glory to God in the highest, and on earth peace, good will toward men."

"Glory! Glory!" can you hear them singing? How the glori- 189
ous melody echoes from mountain to mountain and rolls out
into the farthest reaches of space! "Glory! Glory!" Louder and
louder grows the shout of praise, till it seems all heaven and
earth must hear. Then fainter and fainter and still more
faint as the vision fades, and the shepherds are left alone
with their sheep and the stars again.

Almost two thousand years have passed since then. Two
thousand years! How long the angels have had to wait to see
their dream come true! Jesus did not suddenly save the
world, as they perhaps had hoped. He did not set Himself up
as a king and reign upon the earth. Instead, He let Himself
be led to the cross. And all the while the angels had to stand
by and see their beloved Leader ill-treated and mocked and
beaten and killed. How many times they must have wanted
to step in and save Him from His enemies! And when on one
occasion He told the people that He could if He so wished call
twelve legions of angels to help Him, how they must have
wished that He would do so!

But no, Jesus went to the cross and died, for He knew that
was the only way to bring men back to God.

Many times during His earthly life Jesus told His disciples that after making His sacrifice He would leave them
and come back again someday. He even told them about
some of the signs that would be seen to let them know
when He was about to return. I am sure the angels listened
to every word He said, and that they have been keeping
this promise in their hearts. All these two thousand years
they have been watching for the promised signs, and have
been longing for the day when their Lord and Master shall
come back to the earth and complete His wonderful plans
for those who receive Him.

And they are watching in countries all over the world
to see which boys and girls and men and women are getting
ready to meet Jesus when He comes again.

◀ Painting by Charles Zingaro, © Review and Herald

People all over the world are hearing and an-
swering Jesus' call for them to come to Him.
Are you?

Someday—and it cannot be very far away now—Jesus will return; and when He comes, we are told, "all the angels" will come with Him. Won't that be a wonderful sight! Perhaps you and I will be alive to see it. Who knows? And then, if we are ready, the angels will take us to meet Him in the air. You can almost feel the thrill of it now, can't you? And then, along with the angels, we shall go to heaven to see all the beautiful things that God has prepared for those who love Him.

Painting by Robert L. Berran © by Review and Herald

192 And in that glorious day there will break upon our ears such music as we have never heard—the third wonderful song.

Listen to the triumph song of the angels. It is the song they have been waiting to sing for so long. Their pent-up feelings will find freedom at last in this great chorus. Listen! The lovely strains of melody are coming toward us even now: " 'To him who sits upon the throne and to the Lamb be blessing and honor and glory and might for ever and ever!' " (Revelation 5:13, R.S.V.). For Jesus has won the battle against sin and disease and death.

Finally all that is evil and wicked has been left behind and destroyed. Forever and ever everything will be beautiful, everybody will be happy. Never again will there be any quarreling or fighting or unkind words. Always and always there will be peace and joy and happiness. Forever and ever Jesus will be with His children and they with Him.

Don't you want to join in that lovely song and live in that glorious home? I do. Let's plan to meet there, shall we? And be sure to be ready when Jesus comes.